A SIMPLE AND VITAL DESIGN
The Story of the Indiana Post Office Murals

A SIMPLE AND VITAL DESIGN
The Story of the Indiana Post Office Murals

John C. Carlisle

PHOTOGRAPHY
Darryl Jones

Indiana Historical Society
Indianapolis 1995

Printed in the United States of America

The paper in this publication meets the minimum requirements of American National
Standard for Information Sciences—Permanence of Paper for Printed Library Materials,
ANSI Z39.48-1984. ∞

Library of Congress Cataloging-in-Publication Data

Carlisle, John C.
    A simple and vital design : the story of the Indiana post office
murals / John C. Carlisle : photography by Darryl Jones.
      p. cm.
    Includes bibliographical references.
    ISBN 0-87195-110-X (acid-free paper)
    1. Mural painting and decoration, American—Indiana.   2. Mural
painting and decoration—20th century—Indiana.   3. Indiana in art.
4. Post office buildings—Decoration—Indiana.   I. Indiana
Historical Society.   II. Title.
ND2835.I8C37   1995
758'.99772—dc20   95-10919
                                                      CIP

CITIES, MURAL TITLES, AND ARTISTS   vi

PREFACE   vii

INTRODUCTION   1

INDIVIDUAL MURALS   9

FROM THE PHOTOGRAPHER'S PERSPECTIVE   90

BIBLIOGRAPHY   93

CITIES, MURAL TITLES, AND ARTISTS

Alexandria	*The Sleighing Party*	Roland Schweinsburg
Angola	*Hoosier Farm*	Charles Campbell
Attica	*Trek of the Covered Wagons to Indiana*	Reva Jackman
Aurora	*Down to the Ferry*	Henrik Martin Mayer
Batesville	*Building the Industrial Foundation of Batesville*	Orville Carroll
Boonville	*Boonville Beginnings*	Ida Abelman
Cambridge City	*Pride of Cambridge City*	Samuel F. Hershey
Crawfordsville	*Indiana Agriculture*	Frank Long
Crown Point	*From Such Beginnings Sprang the County of Lake, Indiana*	George Melville Smith
Culver	*The Arrival of the Mail in Culver*	Jessie Hull Mayer
Danville	*Filling the Water Jugs Haymaking Time*	Gail W. Martin
Dunkirk	*Preparations for Autumn Festival, Dunkirk*	Frances Foy
Franklin	*Local Industry*	Jean Swiggett
Garrett	*Clearing the Right of Way*	Joe Cox
Gas City	*Gas City in Boom Days*	William A. Dolwick
Hobart	*Early Hobart*	William A. Dolwick
Indianapolis (Broad Ripple)	*Suburban Street*	Alan Tompkins
Indianapolis	*Mail—Transportation and Delivery; Early and Present Day Indianapolis Life*	Grant Christian
Jasper	*Indiana Farming Scene in Late Autumn*	Jessie Hull Mayer
Knightstown	*The Evening Mail*	Raymond L. Morris
Lafayette	*Rural Delivery; Sad News*	Henrik Martin Mayer
Lagrange	*The Corn School*	Jessie Hull Mayer
Liberty	*Autumn Fields*	Avery Johnson
Ligonier	*Cutting Timber*	Fay E. Davis
Martinsville	*The Arrival of the Mail*	Alan Tompkins
Middlebury	*Early Middlebury Mail*	Raymond Redell
Monticello	*Hay Making*	Marguerite Zorach
Nappanee	*Waiting for the Mail*	Grant Christian
North Manchester	*Indiana Farm—Sunday Afternoon*	Alan Tompkins
Paoli	*Rural Mail Carrier*	Tom Rost
Pendleton	*Loggers*	William F. Kaeser
Rensselaer	*Receiving the Mail on the Farm*	John E. Costigan
Rockville	*Landscape*	Milton Avery
Spencer	*Harvesting*	Joseph Meert
Tipton	*Indiana Farming*	Donald M. Mattison
Union City	*Country Cousins*	Donald M. Mattison

"What mural? Where?"

"Why do you want a picture of that thing?"

More than once I have been asked such questions by patrons or clerks as I sought a good angle for a photograph of the work of art high over the postmaster's office door.

Such "what, where, and why" questions are not too surprising since most of the several hundred murals throughout the country are placed above the postmaster's door, some ten or twelve feet above the lobby floor, and most of these public artworks have been in place for about fifty years. When most people come to the post office, they come to buy a stamp or mail a package, not to look for works of art, and although these customers may have "seen" the mural at one time, by now the paintings have become as much a part of the decorations as the "Wanted" posters which still appear on many small-town post office bulletin boards.

My interest in these works came, almost by accident, in 1969 while searching for information to use in my dissertation on the American artist Ben Shahn. I discovered he had been commissioned in the 1930s by an agency called the Treasury Section of Fine Arts to paint murals for the Bronx Central Post Office and for a smaller post office on Long Island. I was intrigued but not surprised by such information, for I remembered seeing a large wall painting in the lobby of my hometown post office in southern Illinois as a child, but for all I knew back then, that painting was a local aberration. With the realization that my hometown mural apparently represented more than the product of some local artist's whim or fancy, I decided to seek more information on the mural painting program as a sidelight of the dissertation research.

That "sidelight" has become an avocation lasting almost twenty-five years and covering more than twenty-five thousand miles. In that time and over those miles, I have executed statewide surveys in Indiana, California, North Carolina, and Texas, documenting every existing mural produced for a post office lobby in those states between 1934 and 1943, the operating dates of the two programs run by the Section. In addition, I have informal photographs of forty or fifty other locations ranging from Seattle, Washington, to Detroit, Michigan, to Strasburg, Virginia.

"Existing mural" has become the key phrase in my research, for 8 to 10 percent of the murals are gone, victims of deterioration, demolition, or renovation. In addition, some of the buildings that contain the murals now are federal office buildings instead of post offices, some have become the city hall or library or other municipal facility, and some are in private hands, as in the case of one location in California, which housed a liquor store for a brief period.

About a dozen of the murals, on the other hand, have been removed from the lobby walls, refurbished, and placed on more or less permanent loan with local historical societies or colleges and universities, while a few have been moved to new post office buildings. Most of the artworks, however, still occupy their original spot in the lobby, still telling their original stories of a local historical romance or depicting aspects of industrial or agricultural activities in the community.

Even if some of the residents do not always notice the murals, the postmasters are proud of their artworks. I have been in approximately four hundred post offices, and almost without fail, the staff are completely cooperative. Often the postmasters want to share any correspondence they have in their files about the murals, or if the files were sent to Washington, as evidently occurred several years ago in most instances, they want to know what I know about their murals, so they can provide information for the townspeople and visitors who make inquiries.

Without a doubt, during the years I have been conducting my research I have seen a change of interest in and respect for these works of art. One of the purposes I have in writing about these murals is to make more people aware of them, to help anyone interested in Americana and American cultural history to view these murals for the first time or to "see" them once again, this time with a new understanding and perspective.

My commentary, then, is intended, for some readers, as a brief historical introduction to the Treasury's programs and for all readers as a "fieldguide" to the extant Indiana murals, that is, as an aid for those who, like my family and me, will go ten or fifty or one hundred miles out of the way just to see another example of this "New Deal Art."

The essay is a story, too, of the murals, but not necessarily of the muralists. When appropriate and useful, background about the artists is provided along with the discussion of the mural, but focus of the study always is upon the murals. Few "art history" or "art criticism" comments appear here, also, for such is not my purpose; such analyses have been made and will continue to be made by others. At the same time, because this work is not intended as a research tool for scholars, the documentation of material from major research collections such as the National Archives and Records Service, Washington, D.C., the depository of the files of the various art projects around the country, is minimal.

At one time I feared many of the murals all over the country would disappear forever, having been torn off the walls and discarded or painted over, as happened to a few of them many years ago. Now, thanks to national studies such as those done by Marlene Park and Gerald Markowitz and Karal Ann Marling and regional studies such as those done by Barbara Kerr, Peter Bermingham, and Nicholas A. Calcagno, more and more persons are becoming aware of this great national gallery of public art. Although any one mural still may become "temporarily misplaced" for a while as a building changes hands or a mural is reassigned, I am confident most of those in place now, if removed, will be accounted for and preserved or, even better, eventually will show up again, reassigned, refurbished, and reinstalled, once again presenting a view of the "American scene" as it was portrayed by a few hundred artists in the 1930s and early 1940s.

As with any work of this nature, many persons gave assistance and encouragement over the years and were tolerant of my predilections for out-of-the-way artworks—especially my wife Pat and daughters Danielle and Shauna, who must have thought at times that my "avocation" had become an obsession. Richard Guy Wilson gave me my first copy of a Section mural list that he found while digging around in the graduate stacks at the University of Michigan Library when we were students there many years ago. The late Karel Yasko, Counsellor for Fine Arts and Historic Preservation, General Services Administration, always had the latest information about the location of murals and fascinating stories about the trials and tribulations of art preservation in the bureaucracy. This work, too, is a way to say "Thank You" to Dr. Betty Ch'Maj, American Studies scholar, who first introduced me to the fascinating world of interdisciplinary American culture research. This book is dedicated, then, to these friends and loved ones.

John C. Carlisle

On 22 July 1937 Edward B. Rowan, superintendent of the Treasury Department's Section of Painting and Sculpture in Washington, D.C., wrote to Joe Cox, an artist living at 3671 Birchwood Avenue in Indianapolis. In his letter Rowan invited Cox to submit sketches of a mural to be placed on the wall above the postmaster's door in the lobby of the Garrett, Indiana, post office. The letter contained praises for the designs Cox had submitted to the Section in an earlier mural competition and indicated he would be paid $530 for the required 12′ x 4′6″ canvas needed for the lobby space in Garrett. If one of his drawings met Section specifications relative to design and content, he would be given a commission to execute the artwork.

In one of the final paragraphs of his letter, Rowan mentioned two key tenets of the Section's program. He told Cox: "It is suggested that you use subject matter which embodies something appropriate to the building or to the particular locale of Garrett. . . . What we want most is a simple and vital design."[1]

In order to understand fully the importance of this letter to Joe Cox, to American art history, and to the history of American culture, we must look back a few years to Thursday, 24 October 1929, often referred to as "Black Thursday."

THE CRASH

The stock market crash in 1929 signaled more than an end to the Jazz Age Twenties. It was the harbinger also of the Depression Thirties, a time of great changes, great challenges, and—ironically—great successes for some. Between Thursday, 24 October, and Wednesday, 13 November 1929, the stock market lost thirty billion dollars, "a sum almost as great as the entire cost to the United States of its participation in the World War, and nearly twice as great as the entire national debt."[2]

American popular culture lore contains many stories of stockbrokers and bankers jumping from skyscraper windows during those dark days, along with tales of chauffeurs and clerks—who by buying on margins and using paper profits had become players on the market—being wiped out economically and socially in a few days, if not in a few hours. As the "slide" in prices became permanent, many American writers and artists of the "Expatriate" generation of the Twenties began to return from their exhilarating days in Paris. The fortunes that had been made in the market and that had supported their ventures into the studios of the abstract artists and the salon of Gertrude Stein disappeared.

Although the ballooning stock market had pulled in unusual investors such as taxi drivers and librarians, for most "average" Americans—laborers, factory workers, and teachers—the debacle of Wall Street was as much an abstraction as those canvases being produced in Paris. Yet within two years more than one hundred thousand businesses, large and small, had failed because of that whirlpool of worthless stocks and bonds. As historian Milton Meltzer recalled, "By my last year in high school, 1932, one-fourth of the nation—men, women, and children—belonged to families with no regular income."[3] Ironically, two segments of the population were affected only indirectly by the economic troubles of the market: farmers and artists.

For the farmers the entire decade of the 1920s had been one of bad times and falling prices. They had been in no position to dabble in the balloon stock market and, thereby, had little to lose in 1929, for the time being at least.

Art by American artists and with American themes had finally begun to find acceptance among the official critics and tastemakers in the late 1920s, especially the artists who responded to an increasing call for realism. But, as Barbara Rose pointed out, "With the coming of the Depression, what little serious interest there had been in art would soon be distracted by the more pressing issue of the country's economic collapse."[4]

THE NEW DEAL

When Franklin Delano Roosevelt was elected president in November 1932 the Constitution still required a wait until the following March before he could be inaugurated. However, once in office he spearheaded a flood of legislation created to pull the country out of its economic doldrums through reorganization of the banking laws, financial assistance for farmers, and "pump priming" projects designed to provide immediate employment for the millions whose jobs had been lost.

In the first weeks of the Roosevelt administration, a period now referred to as "the 100 days," an "alphabet soup" of new agencies and bureaus was created. The Public Works Administration (PWA), the Civilian Conservation Corps (CCC), the Farm Credit Administration (FCA), the Tennessee Valley Authority (TVA), the Agricultural Adjustment Administration (AAA), and the National Recovery Administration (NRA)—with its national symbol of hope, the Blue Eagle, which shopkeepers posted in their windows—all appeared between 9 March and 16 June 1933.

Contemporary social critics and revisionist historians sometimes disparage the motives behind those efforts, but American artist Ben Shahn recalled those days more positively:

> However depressed human affairs may have been, the human being was likely to be looked upon as a person, an individual; he was hungry or roofless and he had to be helped; that was the new responsibility of his government. I think that it was neither cynical, power-hungry nor calculated to offset unrest; it was simply that old-fashioned word, humanitarian.[5]

Although the unemployed artists in the country at the beginning of the New Deal accounted for less than 1 percent of the total idle workforce, two of the new agencies, the Federal Emergency Relief Administration (FERA) and the Civil Works Administration (CWA), both directed by Harry Hopkins, did provide jobs for artists. When asked to justify creating jobs for this segment of the society, whom most Americans had never considered to be "workers," Hopkins replied, "Hell! They've got to eat just like other people."[6]

What most people did not realize was the federal government had been a "patron" of the arts for a long time, usually through the commissions for occasional murals and sculptures issued by the supervising architect of the Procurement Division of the Treasury. For years the government had supported the plastic arts in this way, but only indirectly did it support the artists.

THE PUBLIC WORKS OF ART PROJECT

On 8 December 1933 the Treasury Department's Advisory Committee on Fine Arts, along with its invited guests Eleanor Roosevelt and the directors of eight of the major art museums in the country, met in the Washington, D.C., home of Edward Bruce, the committee secretary, to develop plans for the employment of artists. "The meeting was called at one o'clock P.M. and lasted until five o'clock P.M., and by the time it was over The Public Works of Art Project was an actuality." The Civil Works Administration allocated $1,039,000 for the Public Works of Art Project (PWAP) "under the Treasury Department as one of the agencies to extend relief to the professional class, its object being to employ artists who were unemployed in the decoration of public buildings and parks."[7]

When Hopkins committed CWA funds for work relief of artists, the logical administrative location for those funds was the Treasury, which had at least some experience in dealing with artists and art commissions through the activities of the supervising architect. Under the program skilled artists and craftsmen would be paid salaries ranging from $26.50 to $42.50 per week. However, before they could be hired they had to meet a "dual test" of eligibility: "First that they were actually in need of the employment, and second, that they were qualified as artists to produce work which would be an embellishment to public property."[8]

Only four days after the Advisory Committee met, the first artists were hired as part of the PWAP, directed by Edward Bruce. Both the CWA and the PWAP were intended as temporary measures during the winter, with 15 February 1934 originally set as the termination date of the programs.[9] The two-month period proved the value of a program for artists, but it provided neither enough time to evaluate the programs nor enough time for many of the artistic projects to be completed. Thus PWAP funding was extended until 28 April 1934, with a few artists later transferred briefly to another program just long enough to complete their projects.

The PWAP was controlled by sixteen regional committees, each with a prominent person from the arts community as director. Indiana was part of Region 9, headed by William Milliken, director of the Cleveland Museum of Art. Although the PWAP records in the National Archives are sketchy as to names and locations of the artists employed, it is known that when the PWAP ended officially with the end of the fiscal year on 30 June 1934, Indiana, Ohio, Kentucky, and Michigan artists had been paid a total of $22,421.08 as wages from the $25,226.23 allocated for Region 9. Nationally, almost four thousand artists received employment, with 90 percent of the funding going directly to the artists as wages.[10]

Even with its short-lived duration, the PWAP proved that the need for financial support of artists existed and that such a large program could be administered by the federal government. Two key concerns that would affect all later art programs—relief and artistic ability—did surface in those few weeks. What the PWAP did not provide was the answer to this problem. How could aid be provided while rigid standards of artistic excellence were upheld?

LATER PROGRAMS

One of the concerns of the New Deal agencies was how to provide aid to needy persons while avoiding direct relief, that is, the dole, which usually meant only small cash allotments plus food tickets. Although, as Ben Shahn said, such "humanitarian" assistance helped the unfortunate individual or family, it did little to boost the economy and thereby put unemployed persons back to work as businesses and factories reopened or returned to earlier levels of production. In addition, the psychological benefits of a job, as opposed to what was perceived as the debilitating effects of the dole, were needed to provide a beneficial boost to the morale of a depressed nation.

When the Works Progress Administration (WPA) was established in 1935, it created a Division of Professional and Service Projects with four programs: art, music, literature, and drama. The Federal Art Project (FAP) was the program designed to promote the production of art and the participation in art events by persons not often exposed to such experiences in order to bring about a positive change in the public view of art, especially the visual arts. The largest of all the art programs, the FAP employed about five thousand persons at one point in its different areas: creation of art, art education, art applied to community services, and technical and archaeological research. Even though the FAP was the largest visual arts project during this time, it had only a small impact upon Indiana.

Although the FAP administrators assumed those eligible for employment had, at least, some modicum of artistic skill, the major criterion for selection was financial need. Holger Cahill, FAP director, "operated under the assumption that large production . . . could bring the desired changes. He was inclined to leave judgment of the quality of the work to posterity."[11] The FAP continued until 1942 when it became the Graphic Section of the War Services Board; all funding was terminated at the end of the 1943 fiscal year.

The Treasury Relief Art Project (TRAP), also created in 1935 with funds from the WPA, functioned under the same employment guidelines as the other WPA programs: 90 percent of the workers were supposed to come from relief rolls, and the monthly wage was $69 to $103 for ninety-six hours of work, with some persons allowed up to one hundred twenty hours. A master artist who employed artists from the relief rolls as assistants supervised each project.[12] These TRAP teams executed murals and sculptures for existing federal buildings and for federal housing projects. In addition, TRAP workers also painted several thousand easel paintings for various government institutions and embassies until funding was withdrawn at the end of fiscal year 1939.

Indiana had four artists employed under the auspices of the TRAP, including Grant Christian as master artist, and a "mural assistant," who met the relief requirements. They painted several scenes of early and contemporary Indianapolis in the corridor outside the third-floor courtroom in what is now the Federal Building in downtown Indian-

apolis; back then it was the main post office as well as a courthouse. A carpenter also worked for two weeks on that project, presumably to install moldings around the canvases. An easel painter in Crawfordsville was given a one-month contract, while the fourth person, a "woodblock maker" in Indianapolis, was employed for sixteen months.

THE SECTION

Approximately four months after all funding was withdrawn from the PWAP in the summer of 1934, Henry Morgenthau, Jr., secretary of the treasury, issued a directive establishing a Section of Painting and Sculpture "to secure suitable art of the best quality for the embellishment of public buildings."[13]

Edward Bruce, who had directed the brief, somewhat experimental PWAP efforts, was chosen to head the new arts program, this one also under the direction of the Treasury but without funding from the WPA and without the constraints attached to the relief programs.

Bruce wanted to help in the dissemination of art throughout the country—such experiences would raise the cultural taste of the citizens—but unlike Cahill, who was willing to leave the question of artistic quality to time, Bruce had "strong convictions about what constituted 'good' art, and artists who worked for the Treasury had to meet his technical and aesthetic standards."[14] Those standards, admirable though they were, precipitated much critical correspondence between artists and the Washington office of the Section during the years 1934 to 1943.

If Bruce and the other members of the Section staff were to achieve their goal of raising public taste through "exposure to consistently good art," that art had to be in easily accessible locations. At that time the Public Building Service, which was in charge of all construction projects for the federal government, was located in the Treasury Department. One of the major construction projects funded by the New Deal Congress included the erection of new post office buildings in many communities throughout the country.

Historically, the post office, whether in a large city or in a small town, has served as the most public of all public buildings. Almost everyone visits this building occasionally, either to pick up mail, purchase stamps, or mail packages. On 2 November 1938 Edward Bruce wrote to President Roosevelt:

With more than forty-five thousand post offices in the country, and an estimated daily attendance of five hundred in each, [this program will carry] out your dream of letting the simple people all over the country see at least one thing of beauty.[15]

Art works such as murals or wall-mounted sculptures in the lobby of a post office would be seen by practically all the residents of a town at one time or another and could be seen repeatedly over the years. Although the Section did commission art for buildings other than post offices, including several office buildings in Washington, D.C., its major effort was expended on work for post office lobbies. While both wall-mounted reliefs and freestanding sculptures were commissioned, most of the works are wall murals, usually mounted over the postmaster's door.

Thirty-seven mural commissions were executed for Hoosier post offices, with thirty-six of them remaining today. The first mural installation was Henrik Martin Mayer's two vertically oriented canvases, 3' x 7'6", *Sad News* and *Rural Delivery* in July 1936 in Lafayette. Marguerite Zorach's 14'6" x 8'6" *Hay Making,* installed in Monticello in November 1942 was the last. The "boom years" were 1938 with twelve murals and 1939 with nine new art works in Indiana post office lobbies.[16]

In view of the fact Bruce was given no official budget with which to pay artists, that art of any kind was produced is amazing, much less the "quality" work he sought. Money for commissions to the artists came from the construction appropriations for the buildings. The Section secured agreement from the Public Building Service that up to 1 percent of the cost of the building could be "reserved" for payment to artists for "embellishment." Not all new buildings had such reserves, but in today's world of cost overruns the fact that approximately fourteen hundred building projects for new post offices did have funds available is astounding.

This procedure of including the artistic costs in the construction budget also helped to protect the Section from the kind of congressional criticism that was the bane of other programs, such as the Federal Theatre Project, often criticized for producing "leftist" drama, or the Federal Art Project, castigated for employing artists who sometimes painted abstract and, perhaps thereby, "un-American" paintings. Even if a proposed post office building might contain a mural or a sculpture, no congressman was going to vote against a new structure for his district nor, in the time-honored practice of politics, was he going to vote against other buildings in other districts.

Another protection against criticism came with the artist selection procedure the Section used—a series of open competitions, open, that is, to artists "born or residing in a locale, state, or region," to use the words of one Section press release. These regional or sectional competitions were designed to comply with another of Secretary Morgenthau's original objectives, that of commissioning local talent for the murals or sculptures "so far as consistent with a high standard of art. . . . In a word, we look to what we have called our 'local' projects for the discovery and development of hitherto comparatively unknown artists."[17]

For Indiana almost one-half of the artists who received commissions—fourteen of twenty-nine—met those residency requirements, although some of them, especially those who were instructors at the John Herron Art Institute in Indianapolis, might not have appreciated the "unknown artist" appellation. Ten of the artists who received Section assignments lived in Indiana at the time of the award, eight in Indianapolis, one in Bloomington, and one in New Albany. Alan Tompkins was teaching at the Herron school when he received the first of his three Indiana commissions, but had moved on to the Cooper Union Art School in New York City by the time he received the last. Three other commissioned artists were born in Indiana.

On the other hand, if the building or the location warranted, that is, had an allocation of more than five thousand dollars, the Section would ignore "geographical limits" and conduct a national competition. All told, between 1934 and 1943, 190 state, regional, and national competitions were held that involved 15,426 artists who submitted 40,426 sketches.[18]

The most massive competition effort came from the "48-State Competition" in 1939. For this contest one post office in each state was selected, with artists invited to submit designs for that particular building in "the largest mural competition every held in America. . . . Forbes Watson, adviser to the Section, described the competition as having brought 'a great big breath of fresh air into American painting.' "[19] Artists were not limited to one building in their submissions, and judges were not limited to selecting a winning design only from those submitted for that particular post office.

Ironically, it was not a native-born artist's sketch that was chosen for Spencer, the Indiana post office designated for the 48-State Competition. In fact, the winning design by Joseph Meert, who lived in Kansas City, Kansas, was proposed by him for the Seneca, Kansas, post office.[20]

With approximately fourteen hundred buildings receiving Section-administered decorations in the nine-year period of its existence, a contest could not be held for each building. Rather, when a typical competition was opened, the Section's announcement stated that the winner would receive a commission for a specific building, while artists whose drawings received an honorable mention could receive contracts for other, smaller buildings, usually in the same geographic area.

Artists submitted their sketches with their names in a sealed envelope attached to the back of the drawing; these works were numbered as they arrived so that the winning work could be designated by number. Once all the anonymous sketches had been received, either in Washington or in the local post office, the selection jury would gather to make its decisions. For the national competitions, nationally known artists and sculptors were asked to serve on the juries, but for smaller competitions, those involving artists in only three or four states, the jury often was composed of the postmaster, a representative of the architectural firm, and other prominent citizens. Their selections plus the non-chosen sketches, with the unopened-but-numbered envelopes still attached to the canvases, were all sent to the Section's office in Washington, where the final choice was made by the Section staff. In only a handful of cases did the Washington staff either question or reject the local selections, and when such rejection occurred, it usually involved the two main controversies of the mural program—"painting Section" and "local chauvinism."

When the Section's *Bulletin* announced competitions, artists who wished to do so and who had developed a certain political savvy about government-funded murals wrote to the postmasters for information about the towns and their histories for leads in developing the content of their sketches. Some artists later told art historian Erica Beckh Rubenstein that they then "painted Section."[21] That is, they submitted sketches of covered wagons arriving in the wilderness or designs depicting famous building and geographical features or scenes lauding the delivery of the mail, all to boost their chances of being selected by a local jury. On the other hand, quite logically, if a local jury had twenty sketches from which to select and if ten of them favorably reflected the town's history or its industrial and agricultural development, town pride often dictated that the three or four sketches selected as winners would be from artists whose work would reflect the most positive aspects or characteristics of the town.

For artists like Alan Tompkins such sketches reflected the appropriate value system of the community. "Generally the ideas came, on my part, from visiting the locales like Martinsville and trying to get a feel of the town, what the people were like, what kind of people they were, farmers or tradesmen or whatever, and doing a mural which seemed to me at that time to suit the surroundings, to suit the post office there."[22] On the other hand, sometimes the need to satisfy local de-

mands had its humorous side. When William Kaeser was developing designs for Pendleton, he submitted one with a grain elevator, the railroad, and wagons unloading grain, a "terrific composition" in his eyes. However, the postmaster said: "I'm not going to advertise that guy's grain elevator." Kaeser then proposed the more general logging scene now on the wall.[23]

Some critics of the program felt this painting to local chauvinism was a limiting factor in the development of quality work,[24] that the artists withheld their best designs, possibly the more progressive or modern designs, because they feared the conservative juries would reject such proposals. Regardless of the degree of truth in the "painting Section" or "local chauvinism" charges, in retrospect, designing to support and satisfy local desires does not seem inappropriate. After all, the mural was to be on a wall in a specific location frequented by a specific clientele. Why not paint a scene that would have meaning to the local inhabitants?[25]

Whatever the specific design elements artists used in a proposal sketch, they were supposed to evoke what often is called "the American Scene," that is, a realistic American subject matter, what Matthew Baigell calls "an interest in topicality, in anecdote, and in local custom."[26] However, this "American Scene" or "American scene" (with no capital "S") label often causes more confusion than clarification. Does it have anything to do with style, especially that style frequently associated with works by Thomas Hart Benton, John Steuart Curry, and Grant Wood, who were labeled "Regionalists"? If so, how were the local artists supposed to respond?

> This extreme position, which came to be called the American scene movement, put an unavoidable burden on the more moderate artist, whose regionalism was not solely a function of artistic nationalism. The bitterness engendered by the right-wing American scene argument would becloud any understanding of the broader nature of regionalism for years to come.[27]

Perhaps the best rule was no rule at all. "The Section did not, as the Public Works of Art Project did, specify American Scene painting as a model for artists, but most of its works fall into that category simply because they were representational and had America, past or present, as a subject."[28] The Section did, however, strongly suggest local scenes and events as primary content considerations even if the official imprimatur was not placed on "American Scene." This viewpoint led to "a contemporary American realism that was natural, authentic, and normative."[29]

Those artists whose commissions came as a result of an honorable mention in a competition—and the overwhelming majority of commissions came as a result of such runner-up status or in a few cases because of previously well-executed murals—developed murals within the content guidelines, but the procedure they followed was, in some ways, more arduous than that followed by the winners. The Section's invitation letter to an honorable mention winner, asking the artist to submit designs for a new mural, often contained the suggestion that he or she go to the new location to talk with the postmaster and others about the history of the town, its industrial/agricultural base, or its local heroes. Whenever possible, most of the artists willingly made such visits, but for someone living in Los Angeles, New Orleans, or New York, such a visit to an Indiana location often was economically impossible.

For example, in 1938, on the basis of outstanding designs submitted for the Department of the Interior Building competition, Antol Shulkin, an artist living in upstate New York, was asked to submit sketches for a mural in Dunkirk, Indiana. Shulkin repeatedly postponed the required trip to the Midwest, citing other commitments that demanded his attention, all the while continuing to submit designs for other national contests. Two years later he asked to be moved to another assignment, one closer to home. The Section agreed, telling him that if something more convenient appeared he "may be asked" to submit designs for that project.

Even if a trip to the site was impossible, the Section at least expected contact be made with the postmaster for the appropriate information. Once an artist had visited a location or had corresponded with a postmaster, two or three pencil sketches of possible mural designs were sent to the Section. Only when one of the sketches had been approved by the Section could a formal commission be offered to the artist, and many times artists had to resubmit proposals or develop new proposals before satisfying the Section staff. With the submission and approval of a color sketch drawn to two-inch scale, the artist was paid one-third of the contracted amount and was told to submit canvas samples along with a list of the kind of oils or tempera paints that would be used.

Then the artist could begin the next step, the preparation of a full-size "cartoon," that is, a pencil drawing on paper. Once an 8″ x 10″ photograph of the cartoon was submitted and approved, the artist was paid a second one-third installment. Approval of the cartoon also meant the artist could begin the actual painting of the canvas.

Usually the Section also required photographs of the canvas when it was half finished.

Other times, especially in the cases of those who had done satisfactory work before, the artists went straight from cartoon to completed canvas, but even for those experienced persons final approval of the canvas was not given until another 8″ x 10″ photograph of the finished work was sent off to Washington. Somewhere between the approval of the cartoon and the approval of the photograph of the finished but not installed mural, the Section staff began the paperwork necessary to secure permission for the artist to install the mural. Only after the Post Office Department had given such approval was the artist allowed to take the canvas to the post office for attachment to the wall, and then only with a cement whose formula had been approved by the Section. Finally, when the artist sent still another 8″ x 10″ photograph, this time of the installed mural, and when the local postmaster sent a letter to the Fourth Assistant Postmaster General in Washington, D.C., confirming the mural had been installed and was satisfactory, the artist was given the final one-third installment of the contract.

The correspondence files now in the National Archives in Washington, D.C., contain many copies of letters between the Section and artists with very specific design suggestions, for example, demanding that certain figures be moved more into the foreground or the background or that the artist find live models for the persons and animals being depicted. On the other hand, the suggestion might be more general, as in the 2 March 1938 letter from Rowan to Alan Tompkins about the sketch for the North Manchester mural, *Indiana Farm—Sunday Afternoon*: "Question was also raised as to whether the farmer's wife would be doing a family washing on Sunday." Eight days later Tompkins wrote back to Rowan: "I have . . . changed her occupation to that of putting a pudding dish in the oven for Sunday night supper. I think this change will be equally successful as design and that it will clear up the inconsistency of subject I had not noticed."[30]

With all these lockstep procedural details and approvals required by the Section—a paperwork flow that often seems adverse to the creative approach of an artist—the fact that many months and, in a few instances, years passed from the time the first sketches were mailed off to Washington to the time a mural appeared on the wall is no surprise. Ironically, however, for the researcher today, without those nit-picking letters and, especially, the 8″ x 10″ photographs, the stories of these murals could not now be told, particularly in regard to those murals that have been destroyed, for the photographs are the only remaining evidence of their existence, as in the case of Walter Gardner's *Christmas Morning Mail* in Berne.

CONCLUSION

Occasionally the persons depicted in post office murals, whether in Indiana or elsewhere, are specific figures, whether fictional, such as " 'The Raggedy Man' who tends the horses 'n feeds 'em hay," the James Whitcomb Riley character featured in Roland Schweinsburg's *The Sleighing Party* in Alexandria or nonfictional, such as Boardman Robinson and Chief Mewonitoc in George Melville Smith's Crown Point mural *From Such Beginnings Sprang the County of Lake, Indiana.* The other people shown may not be identifiable by name, but by type they represent the essence of the American scene concept. They are the farmers, the loggers, the railroad men, the pioneer mothers, and the workers of our history. These are self-made persons, a true grassroots America. As a janitor in the Bronx Post Office told Ben Shahn when he completed his mural series there, "Your putting workers in overalls up there sure will make it easier to organize the men around here."[31] An Indiana postmaster told the author the story of local residents who insisted they knew just the hill where the artist stood to paint a particular landscape, even though the scene actually was a composite of several places in the area and could not have been created from one spot.

In the first issue of the Section's *Bulletin* on 1 March 1935 C. J. Peoples, director of procurement for the Public Works Branch, gave the Section's philosophy:

Without being sentimental, the Section of Painting and Sculpture hopes that in employing the vital talents of this country, faith in the country and a renewed sense of its glorious possibilities will be awakened both in the artists and in their audiences, and that through this the Section will do its full share in the development of the art and the spiritual life of the United States of America.[32]

This was the America and the Americans the Section wanted depicted on the walls of the hundreds of federal buildings being decorated through their efforts during those years at the end of one decade and the beginning of another. Success was theirs—even with the occasional administrative blunder or an unhappy postmaster or two or a disgruntled local editorial writer—and it was a success built,

ironically, upon an economic disaster, the Great Depression, with its concomitant need to find worthwhile employment for hundreds of out-of-work artists.

Four years after its establishment, the Section of Painting and Sculpture changed its name to the Section of Fine Arts, and it was given "permanent" status, seemingly in recognition of its achievements. Less than one year later another change occurred. The Public Building Service of the Treasury was renamed the Public Buildings Administration (PBA) and was placed under the jurisdiction of the new Federal Works Agency. The Section of Fine Arts, now minus the "Treasury" appellation, became a part of the PBA. None of these changes seriously affected the Section's ongoing embellishment efforts. In fact, the only major change that affected the Section was the one that affected all the New Deal programs—war.

When President Roosevelt presented his budget message to Congress in January 1941 he recommended cuts in all nondefense construction projects. Without new buildings to decorate the Section of Fine Arts slowly ceased functioning as an active force in the American art world, although some artists did not complete their projects until several years later. Thus, the records for a few of the mural projects are incomplete, lacking the "final reports" and "letters of installation" submitted by both the artists and the postmasters after a mural canvas had been affixed to the wall. By the time the work in such cases had been completed, 1946 or 1947 for example, there was no place to send the reports, for no agency existed that was interested in knowing the murals had been installed.

Many of the artists employed by the various federal art programs of the 1930s, whether the Section, FAP, or TRAP—artists such as Peter Hurd, Ben Shahn, Paul Cadmus, Jackson Pollack, and Wilhem de Kooning—became major figures in the history of American art. Their employment, whether as muralists in post office lobbies and courthouses or as easel painters, gave them exposure and experience as well as income during difficult times. When the federal patronage ended, the artists who had received mural commissions had to find other employment, and many of them seem to have disappeared from the art scene; today some are virtually unknown.

Regardless of what happened to these artists in later years, their work lives on in hundreds of lobbies, still performing a traditional function of public art—portraying important stories of the towns and of the townspeople of the American scene, thereby celebrating common cultural aspirations and social values.

NOTES

1. For simplicity, all information from "Records of the Public Building Service," Record Group No. 121, National Archives and Records Service, the depository of the files of the federal art projects, will be noted hereafter only as NARS.

2. Frederick Lewis Allen, *Since Yesterday* (New York: Bantam, 1961), 20.

3. Milton Meltzer, *Violins and Shovels: The WPA Art Projects* (New York: Delacorte, 1976), 3.

4. Barbara Rose, *American Art since 1900: A Critical History* (New York: Praeger, 1967), 113.

5. Letter to author, 14 Feb. 1969.

6. Karal Ann Marling, *Wall-to-Wall America: A Cultural History of Post-Office Murals in the Great Depression* (Minneapolis: University of Minnesota Press, 1982), 42, and Marlene Park and Gerald Markowitz, *Democratic Vistas: Post Offices and Public Art in the New Deal* (Philadelphia: Temple University Press, 1984), 5.

7. NARS, RG 121.

8. Ibid.

9. Ibid.

10. Francis V. O'Connor, *Federal Support for the Visual Arts: The New Deal and Now* (New York: New York Graphic Society, 1969), 21.

11. Richard D. McKinzie, *The New Deal for Artists* (Princeton, N. J.: Princeton University Press, 1973), xi.

12. O'Connor, *Federal Support for the Visual Arts,* 25.

13. Section of Painting and Sculpture, Public Works Branch, Procurement Division, Treasury Department, *Bulletin,* No. 1 (1 Mar. 1935), 3.

14. McKinzie, *The New Deal for Artists,* xi.

15. NARS, RG 121.

16. Five sculpture commissions were awarded for Indiana towns as well: Bedford, Bloomfield, Fowler, Indianapolis (downtown), and Tell City.

17. Section of Painting and Sculpture, *Bulletin,* No. 1, pp. 3, 4.

18. A 27 Jan. 1941 article in *Life* magazine commented on Bruce's administrative abilities: "Small but important proof of Bruce's efficiency is that out of thousands of designs sent to him, none was ever mislaid or lost." "America Sees Itself in New Government Murals," 42.

19. "Winners in Government's '48-States Competition' Shown at Corcoran," *The Art Digest,* 15 Nov. 1939, p. 12.

20. As will be shown later, Meert had to make significant changes in his design before it was acceptable to the residents of Spencer.

21. McKinzie, *The New Deal for Artists,* 55.

22. Interview with author.

23. Interview with author.

24. McKinzie, *The New Deal for Artists,* 54.

25. In 1980 Luis Jiminez commented upon changes he was making in a sculpture commissioned by the federal government for a Fargo, North Dakota, location. "I don't want to sound like a commercial artist, but it's entirely different when you're working with a community. The work belongs to the people. It has to come from the artist, but the people have to be able to identify with it." *The Cultural Post,* Issue 23 (Mar./Apr. 1980).

26. Matthew Baigell, *The American Scene* (New York: Praeger, 1974), 16.

27. Rick Stewart, *Lone Star Regionalism: The Dallas Nine and Their Circle* (Austin: Texas Monthly Press, 1985), 38.

28. Park and Markowitz, *Democratic Vistas,* 139.

29. Ibid., 129.

30. NARS, RG 121.

31. John D. Morse, "Ben Shahn: An Interview," *Magazine of Art* (Apr. 1944): 136-41.

32. NARS, RG 121.

Although he did not know it at the time, Roland Schweinsburg inadvertently found the topic for his mural the day he arrived to visit the post office in Alexandria, for the weather was bitter cold and snow covered the ground.

In late November 1937 the Section invited him to submit possible drawings for a mural in Alexandria "on the basis of competent work executed under the Treasury Department Art Projects." As this was the first of three post office murals Schweinsburg would do, the invitation could not be for a past commission. In all likelihood the artist had worked either under a master artist on a TRAP program or he had submitted excellent drawings in an open competition for a different mural. The Washington staff, always on the lookout for competency, decided to make him the offer.

After all, an offer such as this involved no commitment from the Section; if the Section did not like the drawings an artist supplied, it simply offered no contract. If it liked some of the work but wanted changes, it suggested those changes. Only when the sketches satisfied the Section did it issue the formal contract, which still allowed

TITLE
The Sleighing Party

SIZE
11' x 4'3"

ARTIST
Roland Schweinsburg

FEE
$520

BASIS FOR THE AWARD
"Competent work executed under the Treasury Department Art Projects"

MEDIUM
Oil on canvas

DATES
Contract 1 March 1938 for 122 calendar days

Postmaster letter confirming installation, 19 July 1938

LOCATION OF BUILDING
205 West Church Street

the Section to require other content and/or design changes as the work progressed.

Upon receipt of the letter from Washington, Schweinsburg immediately wrote back: "I am very grateful of the opportunity to submit designs for the Alexandria, Ind., P. O. I expect to visit Alexandria Dec. 8th to go over the ground and see the postmaster." Since Schweinsburg lived in Youngstown, Ohio, he decided to take the train to Alexandria, a distance of approximately three hundred miles. "As the train schedules work out," he wrote to Edward B. Rowan, superintendent of the Section, "I will arrive at 12 midnight so I propose to stay overnight in nearby Elwood, 10 miles from there. I will prepare sketches as soon as I have returned from there."

Schweinsburg knew enough about the Section's procedures that he knew the location visit was almost mandatory, and, as he probably was a recipient of the Section's *Bulletin,* he also knew a sketch that promoted the town would be a safe design to submit, even if, as he knew by experience, "it is 'tin and sheetwool country' since a great many people from this section are working there." A few weeks later the pencil sketches, aggrandizing the rock wool industry, were sent to Washington. "There were a few other industries there in Alexandria, but none seemed so vital to the locality as the rock wool."

Here is a case where following the rules brought an unwanted response. On 25 January 1938 Rowan acknowledged receipt of the designs showing the "leading local industry." He added that "your selection of that subject matter is, of course, appropriate. We feel, however, that neither of the designs which you have submitted would be of any real interest or joy to the visitor of the Post Office and for that reason I am asking you to forward some further proposals for the decoration in question."

Two weeks later Schweinsburg had four new sketches in the mail, "one oil, one watercolor and 2 pencil studies. The oil was inspired by James Whitcomb Riley's poem, 'Let's go out to old Aunt Mary's,' an old fashioned sleigh ride scene." He added support for the winter incident when he commented that "Riley worked as a reporter on a nearby Anderson newspaper and is well beloved thruout [*sic*] that section." About the time the mural was installed, Schweinsburg elaborated on his choice in another letter to the Section office. In addition to the fact that Riley was born in "that vicinity" and had worked in Anderson, the artist said he was

inspired by the cold weather when I visited that city. . . . I have taken characters from [Riley's] poems to make up the personnel of

the party, such as the 'Raggedy Man' who 'tends the horses 'n feeds 'em hay,' Old Aunt Mary in the doorway, etc. The period will be about 1900 or shortly after rural free delivery was instituted.

Schweinsburg was a stickler for details, and on 8 June asked for a two-week extension of his contract, even though it did not end until 30 June.

I hesitate to slight any detail of the "Sleighing Party" mural because it's so close to my heart and I want to paint the thing most thoroughly. Such details as snaffles rings . . . on the harness, while of no mural consequence, will be enjoyed by the residenters [*sic*] and make this painting more beloved. In other words they are the Sears Roebuck catalogue searching people and will enjoy this application to detail.

The artist meant his "catalogue searching" comment as a compliment to the folks of Alexandria, not as a pejorative, and the Section staff "greatly appreciated" his "presenting the work in the most thorough manner possible." They were also "confident that the work is not only going to prove an attractive addition to the building  but that it is going to be enthusiastically received by the people of Alexandria."

Apparently both the artist and the Section staff were correct in their efforts and predictions. Schweinsburg's final letter about this mural on 18 July 1938, three days after he and his wife cemented the canvas to the wall, ended with a note of justifiable pride.

I had a lot of fun in listening to the customers' comments on the "Sleigh Ride," especially by the old-timers and incidentally heered [*sic*] some rare Sleigh Ride stories, *not printable.* Everyone seemed to like the painting.

Schweinsburg completed two other post office murals: *Old Bennett Pottery Plant* for East Liverpool, Ohio, in 1937 and *Van Ausdal's Trading Post* for Eaton, Ohio, in 1939.

Few murals in the Indiana post offices caused any controversies, either during their execution or after their installation, but Charles Campbell's efforts in Angola did produce some less than satisfied observers, both in Washington and in Indiana.

Campbell was asked to propose sketches for Angola on the basis of "competent designs" submitted for another competition, a large competition for the Cleveland post office. From the beginning, however, some of his Indiana figures—whether of animate or inanimate objects—bothered the Section staff. For example, in a 23 March 1937 letter Edward B. Rowan cautioned that the scale of the barn and silo in a sketch "seemed to be rather small" in relation to other buildings. In September of that year, at the "half finished stage" of the mural when an additional payment was called for in the contract, Rowan advised the artist that "the stance of the cow, particularly in the relation of the foreleg under her, is not convincing and further study is needed." The little girl on the right also worried Rowan: "In view of her prominence in the foreground of the mural I suggest that you draw her skirts over

TITLE
Hoosier Farm

SIZE
12' x 4'6"

ARTIST
Charles Campbell

FEE
$550

BASIS FOR THE AWARD
"Competent designs submitted in Cleveland competition"

MEDIUM
Oil on canvas

DATES
Contract 29 March 1937 for 300 calendar days

Postmaster letter confirming installation, 17 December 1937

LOCATION OF BUILDING
Mural has been moved to the Community Center, 317 South Wayne Street

her knees as the mural will be bound to be criticized on the basis of immodesty in this minor regard." So, even before the mural was half done, Campbell's buildings scale, his bovine anatomical accuracy, and his sartorial indiscretion had been called into question. All those problems apparently were solved, for no later commentators questioned any of those elements in the painting. What was called into question can be blamed, perhaps, on the efforts of the Section and of the artist to offend no one in the local community, an action that brought a troubling kind of mediocrity.

In his September 1937 letter Rowan referred to "the types which should be fairly pleasant," and by that he meant the "type" of person being portrayed in the mural. "This is a peaceful scene where the individuals have always had plenty to eat and the types which are used in the finished design should reflect this. The little girl on the extreme right still seems especially austere." This insistence upon well-fed farm families is troubling to today's critics, especially when it is realized that Rowan had come to Washington from several years in Iowa and knew that farm families suffered in the depression like many other families. However, the official stance of the Section was to portray "the American Scene" in the post office murals, and that painting genre, with its midwestern, regionalist thrust just did not allow for "austere" figures.

On 27 October Campbell responded to Rowan's criticisms:

The faces on the completed panel are, I believe, as pleasing as I could, with decency make them, without having them vapid. . . . And the cow is now as correct in all ways as I can make it and still give it life. . . . I have lately become something of an authority on cows, their anatomy, movements, and disposition—so I am genuinely glad of the insistence; it definitely added to my education.

In a later letter to Washington, Campbell said the design "has no particular story or historical background." Perhaps still smarting from the earlier reproof, the artist pointed out that

the characters are simple country folk, reasonably prosperous, reasonably contented, and totally lacking in social consciousness. . . .

The dog snarling at the cow is pure barnyard drama and has no symbolic intent, as has been suggested to me by one infected by too much reading of the Social Trend in Art. I mention this merely to forestall any profound interpretation of a wholly innocent panel.

That very innocence seemed to annoy the writer of a 24 November 1937 article in the *Steuben Republican* sent to Washington by the Angola postmaster, who added that "the remarks we hear daily on the post office lobby are much along the same line."

The anonymous reporter and critic began his second paragraph with an almost standard disclaimer: "Not being versed as an artist, we hesitate to attempt the description of the work." Despite the writer's proclaimed lack of requisite training, what followed came close to being a square foot by square foot analysis of the painting. For example, the cow and the dog "are enclosed in a pen about three times as long as the cow and about as wide as the cow is long." Almost as though he were privy to one of Campbell's letters, the newspaper writer called the scene "bucolic—perhaps intended to be typical of a Steuben County farm, and not of any specific location." Perhaps a similar intuitive perception led the writer to call for a scene "more true to Steuben County" than the " 'type' picture which he evidently has tried to produce." In what Shakespeare surely would have called "the most unkindest cut of all," the writer ended with a call for a different allocation of the funds used for the mural:

Perhaps we are not artistically minded in this community, and we venture the assertion that most of the people of Steuben County would have preferred very much that this $600 had been spent in building a modern front that would enclose the steps to the postoffice, which become icy and treacherous in winter.

Charles Campbell painted no other Section murals.

The life story of Reva Jackman and the developmental history of the Attica mural are examples of change and growth applicable to many American artists in the first third of this century and to the Section in the first third of its existence. When Forbes Watson, an adviser in the Section office in Washington, D.C., contacted Jackman for information about the mural in March 1938, shortly before the work was installed in Attica, the artist sent the usual descriptive commentary about the characters and the events taking place in the composition. She said she wanted to portray "the spirit of the pioneers who undertook the difficult task of cross-country travel via the covered wagon." The "young mother" symbolized "the courageous, patient and determined character" of the pioneer woman, who, through it all, retained "a feminine attractiveness and sweetness."

TITLE
Trek of the Covered Wagons to Indiana

SIZE
5' x 4'

ARTIST
Reva Jackman

FEE
$350

BASIS FOR THE AWARD
"Competent design submitted in the Decatur, Illinois, competition"

MEDIUM
Oil on canvas

DATES
Contract 13 December 1937 for 160 calendar days

Postmaster letter confirming installation, 28 May 1938

LOCATION OF BUILDING
100 East Main Street

The immigrant man "embodies the . . . courage, perseverance, and reliability . . . of such men," while the children dream and hope for "their new home to be." The episode is "an imaginative setting without definite place or character in mind . . . in a slightly rolling section of Indiana."

All this is a standard description of a standard American Scene design, not unlike hundreds of others sent to the Section office to describe hundreds of other murals. However, a few days after Jackman wrote the above mural commentary, she sent Watson a biographical sketch that reveals much about her somewhat typical life as an American artist in the first third of the twentieth century.

She could not recall just when she began painting "for I have always (so it seems) been doing it." At the same time, she added, "I have always (since school) worked in an office as a secretary," with instruction in painting only during evenings and weekends, "so that it took many more years than could be accomplished full time." This "work-and-study" routine soon led to discouragement: "For over five years I never touched my paints. But I couldn't leave it alone." About 1923 she returned to night classes, but this time at the Art Institute of Chicago.

"In the spring of 1926 I resigned a secretarial position and went to Paris to study for a year, *full time,* for the first time in my life. What an opportunity!" Apparently she lived rather frugally, for she managed to stretch one year into two and one-half years. "I attended the Julian Academy for a short time, then tried Colorossi and the Grande Chaumiere . . . worked for some time with Andre Lhote, the modernist, [and] painted outdoor scenes in Paris with Frank M. Armington."

Several paintings were exhibited and sold in those years in Paris, followed by other exhibitions and sales in New York and in Wichita, Kansas, her hometown, but by 1935 her primary support came from the various federal art projects around Chicago: PWAP paintings chosen by the Board of Education for their offices and for several schools; a WPA mural, *Characters in Children's Stories,* for the Hawthorne School in Libertyville; and "some work on the Index Dept. [the Index of American Design] in the meantime."

Just as Jackman had modified her plans several times as her training progressed and her artistic abilities improved, so, too, did the Section change and modify its procedures and activities as it matured from its beginning in 1934 to the time of Jackman's Attica commission, that is, during the first third of its being. According to the Attica file in the National Archives, the original 1935 authorization to hold 1 percent for decorative embellishment in the building also called for a local competition, a local selection panel, with "the work of the artist chosen to execute the mural . . . supervised by the chairman and the committee."

Yet the amount of money available for this commission, $350, hardly seemed to justify a competition, especially since by December 1937, when Jackman's contract was signed, the Section was commissioning murals at the rate of one or more a day, often large murals resulting from regional and national competitions. Thus the plans for local competitions, which seemed so logical and easy to conduct when the Section planners mapped the first strategies in 1934, now, just three years later, were not justifiable in terms of the time and money needed to conduct such a competition.

Edward B. Rowan, superintendent of the Section, further justified his ignoring of the original competition and award scheme when he told C. J. Peoples, director of procurement in the Treasury, "all the Indiana artists available from competitions have assignments with the Section." Wanting to forestall any complaints, Rowan added:

> The art interests of Indiana and Illinois are closely allied since the Indiana artists exhibit annually in Chicago and regard that as their center of art activities. The job in question is only $350 and the artist merely goes to her neighboring state to do the work. She could hardly be regarded as an outsider by anyone in Indiana.

Whether because 1938-39 was the busiest time for the Section or because the amount of the commission was so small or because Jackman's artistic abilities were above average—or a combination of all of these—the Attica mural design received only minimal corrective suggestions. When Rowan approved the pencil sketch on 13 December 1937 he felt "the pose of the ox on the left is a little too affected and this might be overcome by enlarging [the] panel slightly on the left or by placing the oxen and the wagon further into the background." With the letter carrying approval of the color sketch came a compliment: "A fine dignity was sensed in the painting of the mother and child and the color throughout is satisfactory. The only suggestion offered is that the man leading the oxen may be slightly stilted and yet romantic in drawing."

Her Attica mural gained for her a second commission, this time for the post office in Bushnell, Illinois, where she installed another story of early life on the prairie, *Pioneer Home in Bushnell,* in 1939.

The generic award comment to the right, "competent work executed under the Treasury Department Art Projects," camouflaged the esteem the Section held for Henrik Martin Mayer. Shortly after his successful dual-panel mural in Lafayette in 1936, the first in Indiana, Mayer won another competition, this one for eight murals in the lobby of the Marine Hospital in Louisville, Kentucky. Then on 27 October 1937, approximately six weeks shy of his thirtieth birthday, he was asked to submit designs that could lead to another commission, for the mural in Aurora.

For the Section Mayer represented a small group of painters who deserved recognition and awards because they combined talent and youth, proving that newer, that is younger, artists were as capable of producing worthy designs as the older group of artists, especially mural painters, who seemed to control the art scene. For example, in an article in the Sunday edition of the *New York Times,* 4 August 1935, Forbes Watson, an adviser to the Section, discussed—or, perhaps, in retrospect, "justified" would be a better term—the new

TITLE
Down to the Ferry

SIZE
12′ x 5′6″

ARTIST
Henrik Martin Mayer

FEE
$915

BASIS FOR THE AWARD
"Competent work executed under the Treasury Department Art Projects"

MEDIUM
Oil on canvas

DATES
Contract 14 February 1938 for 106 working days

Postmaster letter confirming installation, 3 June 1938

LOCATION
501 Third Street

mural painting programs of the Treasury Department. He pointed out that the decoration of federal buildings was a long tradition, an altogether fitting and proper activity carried out over the years in many structures in Washington, D.C., especially in the Capitol and the Library of Congress. The Section's program, which Watson promoted in his article, had two differences: the style of the works and the age of the artists.

He cited the "high spots in the history of mural painting in America in the last forty-odd years," beginning with the Chicago World's Fair in 1893. The "graduates" of that experience "created a kind of mural painting that was peculiar to America. It had a lot of sweetness and light and a kind of pretentious uplift in its glorified and prettified symbolic figures of Law, Justice, Education, Enlightenment and such like abstractions represented in the form of a mural version of American womanhood on a grand scale, all done in a kind of pallid echo of the late Renaissance." Watson then mentioned the work produced by the students from "Charles McKim's pet institution, the American Academy at Rome," but gave his attention next to the work of the Mexican muralists whose art attracted the attention of American artists with a "liberal and radical" inclination.

> The rude protest against our overpolite archaeological schools of mural painting was one cause of their joy. Another came from the recognition that whatever the shortcomings of the Mexicans might be, they did at least use their art as a social expression.

In contrast, at least as Watson perceived the art scene, the "gentlemanly archaeologists" of mural painting in the States ignored the "vulgarities, protests, vicissitudes, conflicts" of daily life while their "architect friends . . . handed choice opportunities to them." All that would change with the Section's requirement for open competitions, which might prove to be a "painful experience" for these older, established artists.

Yet, their maturity may have proven to be valuable after all, for Watson admitted that for the Section, "experience has proved of very great value" for artists seeking commissions. That is, painting a mural means more than painting an easel painting larger. Even the younger, award-winning artists were not "making their debut in mural painting" when they submitted the winning competition designs. He then cited Henrik Martin Mayer's training in mural painting at the Yale School of Art, his work as assistant to a muralist in New York, and his own murals in the Woman's Cosmopolitan Club in New York City. "Both his experience and the studies he has made for Louisville prove

that he is far from being a novice." Watson also cited Tom LaFarge, who "has had, at the age of 31, much more experience than many an older artist," as a prime example of these young but experienced and qualified artists.

Thus, when Rowan contacted Mayer on 27 October 1937 about the possibility of a mural in the Ohio River town of Aurora, the approbation evident in Watson's article evidenced itself again. Ten days later the artist replied that he would submit sketches and included in his note "many thanks to you and the Section for another chance to do some murals in the Ohio River locality."

What followed then was the routine, sometimes tedious, paperwork process needed to proceed in the bureaucracy. Mayer, who may well have visited Aurora while developing his river scenes for the Louisville hospital, developed several ideas specifically for Aurora, chose the best one, and sent the pencil sketch to Washington on 8 January 1938. On 12 January Rowan sent notice of approval to Mayer back in Indianapolis: "The subject matter was regarded as quite interesting and appropriate to the locale. You may proceed with the two inch scale color sketch of this work which is being photographed and will be returned to you under separate cover."

He then outlined for the artist the miscellaneous, but important, details to be provided "in order to enable us to proceed with the writing of your contract."

1. Title of the mural.
2. Exact dimensions of the space to be decorated.
3. Medium in which you will work.
4. Earliest possible date you can complete and install this work.

Also included was a "technical outline," a kind of questionnaire to be submitted by the artist with brand names of art supplies to be used, an indication of experience with preparation of bonding materials for securing the mural to the wall, and a sample of the canvas the artist would use if the work was not a fresco. A month later all the needed facts and figures were in the Section office, and on 14 February 1938 the contract was written for the Aurora mural, *Down to the Ferry,* a 12′ x 5′6″ work to be done in oil on canvas, within 106 working days, for a $915 fee.

Only one critical suggestion came from Washington, and that came at a late date, 30 May, following the completion of the full-sized cartoon:

> [T]he head of the man in the doorway on the right is somewhat crowded in relation to the other two figures. . . . I believe that in

transferring your cartoon to the canvas you could very readily move the figure with upraised hand forward without in any way interfering with your composition. In fact such revision might even improve this area.

On 3 June 1938 the Aurora postmaster wrote the Fourth Assistant Postmaster General. "The mural adds quite a lot to the lobby and I am very well satisfied with the theme of the painting. I have had many favorable comments on the painting from the Public."

What he did not mention and what today's viewers will notice if they try to find the spot where Mayer might have stood to make his original sketch is that such a spot does not exist. That is, for the sake of his composition the artist had to reverse the curve of the river. Mayer's painting came long before the contemporary "Photo-Realism" school of painting, which requires total adherence to reality.

Henrik Martin Mayer also painted both *Sad News* and *Rural Delivery* for Lafayette in 1936.

TITLE
*Building the Industrial
Foundation of Batesville*

SIZE
13'6" x 5'6"

ARTIST
Orville Carroll

FEE
$560

BASIS FOR THE AWARD
*"Competent work executed
under the Treasury Department
Art Projects"*

MEDIUM
*Tempera on gesso (later changed
to tempera on canvas)*

DATES
*Contract 1 June 1937 for 365
calendar days (later changed to
6 November 1937)*

*Postmaster letter confirming
installation, 27 June 1938*

LOCATION
3 West George Street

J ust as Henrik Martin Mayer received praise and support from Forbes Watson in a 1935 article in the *New York Times* because of the work done in the Louisville, Kentucky, Marine Hospital, Orville Carroll received an invitation to submit designs for a mural in Batesville based upon his "competent work executed under the Treasury Department Art Projects," which, in fact, meant other murals in the Louisville hospital. The letter from Edward B. Rowan to Carroll on 5 March 1937 received a reply dated four days later, which assured the Washington office the artist "certainly would like to submit some designs for it," with thanks for "the inspiring confidence you have shown in me."

Perhaps because of that confidence and because Carroll truly wanted to improve his work, the Batesville mural finally was completed satisfactorily, even after many changes, modifications ranging from concrete elements—the surface upon which the artist was to paint—to design problems—"baggy pants" on one figure and architectural features in the original sketches that do not show up in the final painting. This mural, then, can stand as another example of cooperative effort between patron and artist that benefited them and the intended audience, the Batesville post office customers.

A few days after he received the invitation letter, Carroll, who actually lived in New Albany, Indiana, just across the river from Louisville, made the almost mandatory trip to Batesville to talk with the postmaster and other local notables who might give suggestions for design elements, if not for the entire narrative to be told in the mural. Carroll struck a gold mine of Batesville information just by walking into the office of the postmaster.

Carroll told Rowan in a 22 March 1937 letter: "I had a splendid experience in Batesville, Ind. The Postmaster, Mr. Andres, is very enthusiastic about the mural. He had discussed it with several people before I arrived and had quite a lot of photographs of Batesville for me." The artist then went on to tell about the early settlers who came to Batesville in 1832 from Cincinnati "because of the excellent hardwood forests in that neighborhood. They were woodworkers, carvers, cabinet makers and carpenters. This is an enviable background, the real stuff!" A local historian, Mrs. Wyckoff, wrote copy for an advertising brochure for one of the furniture factories in the town, and she made all the photographs she had collected, some dating back to 1878, available to Carroll.

At the bottom of the first page of that 22 March letter, Carroll provided a sketch of one design element that particularly attracted him and commented: "On the houses yet there are carved decorations that run along the top of the porch and up the eaves of the houses. They were very attractive." Ironically this architectural conception that caught his fancy on his first trip to Batesville is the only decorative component in his sketches that was removed due specifically to the Section's critical response.

The questions about his intentions began early on, however, when Alexander Abels, the technical adviser, objected, apparently as soon as he saw the official contract, to Carroll painting on gesso, a kind of pressed wood, rather than on canvas. After several pointed references to the nonstandard surface for the paint, Rowan told Carroll he needed to change to canvas. By September Abels corresponded directly to Carroll: "Thank you for . . . sample of canvas you propose to use on the mural. I find your presentation very good but the cotton canvas is not acceptable. We are requiring a linen canvas to be used on jobs for the Section." The issue of wood versus canvas probably explains why the contract was rewritten in November.

Even while the acceptable surface was being chosen, the design consultants in the Section office, that is, Rowan, Watson, and Edward Bruce, the Section chief, had begun to question the artist's efforts. The color sketch was returned "for further consideration." On 28 July 1937 Rowan wrote: "[W]e frankly feel that the approach is too toy like to carry any degree of authenticity." Although Rowan thought "the figures in themselves . . . quite delightful," the treatment of the trees is "so arbitrary that we do not feel they have much to add to the design." As always, the Washington critics were sticklers for reality. "The horses and cart definitely need further study. It is suggested that you draw a horse from nature and that you authenticate the cart." Reference also occurs to "builders on the left" and their construction methods; whether Rowan meant the bricklayers on the right or whether Carroll changed the scheme to move this part of the design to the other side, we do not know today. No reference remains to the "attractive carved decorations" on the houses Carroll mentioned in his first letter. Perhaps it was the way the Section referred to this element that made Carroll eliminate it: "Also in the matter of the playful architecture we want you to authenticate it as much as possible." The artist probably did not intend to be "playful" when he gave special recognition to these Victorian gingerbread decorative elements, but if Rowan thought it was "playful" then perhaps it should go, for Rowan's letter ended with a strong admonition: "These criticisms, I know, must sound severe to you but we are interested in your doing the best work of which you are capable and we do not feel that you have indicated it in this sketch."

Three or four other long letters went back and forth between New Albany and Washington about the Batesville mural with suggested revisions, some minor, some quite major—move this, change that, check the relationship of this to that—including the last one made on the basis of the photograph of the completed mural just prior to installation: "You might find it helpful to check on the drawing of the [hind quarters] of the horse. The trousers of the figure on the extreme right should be checked particularly the seat as it is a little confusing and somewhat amusing in the present state." Apparently Carroll managed to hitch up the pants a bit because the figure no longer has baggy pants and the cart now more or less hides the horse's hind quarters.

On 27 June 1938 the postmaster wrote that the installation was completed with the exception of a final coat of varnish that Carroll would apply later. With the letter came copies of a story in the local newspaper describing the mural and noting that "Mr. Carroll had three of his students from the Louisville Art Center assist him in the installation of the mural. . . . It is truly a fine piece of work and one which further publicizes the fact that Batesville is a modern, progressive city."

Two months later Carroll wrote to Washington with information about Osceola, Arkansas, where he had gone to prepare sketches for another possible post office mural commission, which he received. The mural, *Early Settlers of Osceola*, was installed in 1939. A third post office mural commission, *Founding of Fort Harrod*, was installed in Harrodsburg, Kentucky, also in 1939.

TITLE
Boonville Beginnings

SIZE
12'7" x 5'6"

ARTIST
Ida Abelman

FEE
$800

BASIS FOR AWARD
"Competent work performed under the Section"

MEDIUM
Casein tempera on canvas

DATES
Contract 2 June 1941 for 271 calendar days

Postmaster letter confirming installation, 28 November 1941

LOCATION OF BUILDING
214 West Locust Street

The "competent work" referred to in the invitation letter to Ida Abelman on 17 March 1941 was the mural she had installed in the Lewistown, Illinois, post office a few weeks earlier. That commission came as a result of her designs submitted in the 48-State Competition in 1938, an abstract layout based upon the development of large steam shovels used in strip-mining coal in the Midwest. Although she did not win the Illinois site award for the 48-State Competition, she was invited to submit designs for Lewistown, historical designs emphasizing the "milestones" of the development of the area from the pioneers to Abraham Lincoln to arrival of the railroad.

When invited to submit designs for Boonville, Abelman again offered a contemporary theme, this time one depicting a merging of industrial development and agriculture, with power lines, antennas, machinery, and cornstalks to show Indiana as the "Crossroads of the Country." To support her visual scheme she attached a lengthy prose explanation on an undated proposal:

> The history of Boonville does not differ fundamentally from that of other pioneer towns throughout the middle West. Like most of

them Boonville has had experiences with Indians, a corduroy road, and gerrymandering politicians.

Boonville became the important town of the county as a result of the coming of the railroad. . . . Boonville exits today, a typical middle-west town exemplifying the progress (and anachronisms) of the American Scene both historical and contemporary.

I feel a mural composed of symbols identifying contemporary intellectual and material forces is appropriate and timely.

Boonville is a part of the vast mining and agricultural area of Indiana. My sketch is so designed as to illustrate the interdependence that exists between one activity and the other . . . dramatic transformation of landscape through mining and agriculture . . . activity under-surface; growth and development on and above surface; transportation, communicating, electrification.

However vigorous Abelman's defense of her composite scheme, once again the Section suggested, rather strongly, that a more historical setting would be desirable.

On 7 May Edward B. Rowan responded to the proposal:

My own feeling is that even though you have presented an abstraction there should be some indication of the local landscape at least as the source of the landscape used in your design. Knowing this region of Indiana I am aware that this has not been achieved.

He ended his letter with this admonition: "In a previous letter I quoted an excerpt from the postmaster's letter and I think it indicates the road you should take, namely a landscape of the pioneer period and a portrait of Ratliff Boon."

On 17 May Abelman defended her choice once more by telling Rowan that the subject of the mural proposal was not "Power's contribution to the cultivation of the land"; the design was intended to "emphasize the interdependence of mining and agriculture, two important activities of the region." She ended the letter with approbation for the Section, adding "I want to clarify this point because I respect the Section's opinion."

Having said all that, she began to develop the suggested historical personality motif for Boonville's post office, using an 1838 statement by Ratliff Boon after his election to the United States Congress:

Twenty-seven years ago, I removed from the State of Kentucky to the then Territory of Indiana, and being at that time unable to make a payment for a lot of land for a home for myself and family, I, like many others, settled upon the public lands with good intentions, when my nearest neighbor was a hostile Indian, and my only shelter from the storm, and my protection from danger was an open camp; and the bark of the elm tree when spread upon the cold earth served both as my floor and my carpet.

The artist told Washington that this was the "theme illustrated in the sketch submitted" and added that she planned "to work 'on location.'" Perhaps her last comment, the "work 'on location'" idea, precipitated some of the heavy amount of criticism of the sketches and drawings Abelman sent to the Section office.

That is, if the artist had painted the canvas in her studio she would have had to submit an 8″ x 10″ photograph of the finished work before authorization would be given to hang the mural. If she worked on site, however, any needed modifications would have to be undertaken in full view of the daily traffic through the post office lobby. No Washington bureaucracy wants to expose its modus operandi like that, so the commentary to the artist is direct, and sometimes blunt, as it relates to figuration and design elements.

On 26 August 1941 Rowan wrote that Abelman's "plow, the fallen tree, the general treatment of the forest and the scout, dog, etc. are

satisfactory. In fact they are well carried out." But the Indian heads were a problem:

> Even we in this office who see hundreds of designs were somewhat startled. . . . The distortion of the cattle is also very questionable as is the head of the figure peeping from the covered wagon and the plane of the man pushing the wheel. . . . This whole area . . . carries too much of the spirit of a caricature of the scene.

The mural in the Boonville post office lobby contains no Indian heads, no figure peeping from the wagon, and no person pushing any wheel. The artist simply eliminated the objectionable elements and adjusted the layout of the design by moving other elements; then she had a workable plan for her mural.

On 15 March 1982 Abelman returned to Boonville for a reception to commemorate the fortieth anniversary of the installation of the mural. During an interview at that time, she pulled out a copy of the original "interdependence of mining and agriculture" design. "And when I came out [to Boonville in 1941] with my sketch and asked these high school kids, the young people who came to the post office [to watch me paint], which they preferred, this or Ratliff Boon, they all seemed to prefer the contemporary theme."

Abelman's relationship with the Section bears one other significant notation. Once the mural was completed in Boonville, Abelman obviously wanted additional commissions and wrote to Rowan asking for such. On 9 December 1941 he responded:

> Relative to your question concerning a further assignment under this program I wish to say that this office, due to the limited number of mural commissions available at this time, has had to adopt the policy of giving further commissions only on the basis of meritorious designs submitted in competitions.

In other words the glory days, when the Section had so much work to assign that there was no need or time for anonymous, juried competitions for every mural, were gone; what commissions would come now, and few did come after Pearl Harbor, would be given only after stiff competition.

Ida Abelman's other mural, *Lewistown Milestones,* was installed in the Lewistown, Illinois, post office, also in 1941.

E dward B. Rowan sent the standard "invitation to submit sketches" letter to Samuel F. Hershey on 2 January 1941; seven days later Hershey wrote to the Cambridge City post-master requesting information about the town, its economic base, and its history. From then until late November when the mural was installed, probably no Indiana post office mural artist tried harder than Hershey to satisfy both patron—the Section of Fine Arts in Washington—and client—the Cambridge City postmaster—as he labored on what proved to be an outstanding artwork.

I. J. L. Harmeier, the postmaster, responded to Hershey's note with a full-page, single-spaced letter of information about the city:

> As to our community activity and history, we are located on national Highway U.S. 40, the old National Road, which is historically and actually at present, one of the most important highways of the nation.

TITLE
Pride of Cambridge City

SIZE
9′6″ x 4′6″

ARTIST
Samuel F. Hershey

FEE
$750

BASIS OF THE AWARD
Designs submitted in Social Security Building Competition

MEDIUM
Oil on masonite board; later changed to oil on canvas

DATES
Contract 16 June 1941 for 167 calendar days

Postmaster letter confirming installation, 27 November 1941

LOCATION OF BUILDING
227 West Main Street

We have ten or eleven factories manufacturing caskets, wood folding chairs, prepared stock feed, and heavy metal rolls and shears used internationally in working heavy metal sheets.

We are in the center of a very fine agricultural area in which corn, hogs and dairy products predominate. We also produce small grains such as wheat, oats and rye. . . .

The race-horse industry has been a prominent feature in past days of Cambridge City, this town having been the seat of the annual sales of the Lackey family, a tradition in the community for many years. More recently, the city produced "Single G," the world's record pacing horse, just recently deceased. . . .

We are also on the TWA air line and hope in the future to have regular pick-up services.

Many of those items appear in the mural in some way or another, but the artist tried to get the postmaster to prioritize them since no canvas could hold all that information. Hershey's request for "what the community would appreciate having brought out" elicited another full-page, single-spaced reply:

(a) The location, being on modern U.S. Highway No. 40, has seen the development of transportation from the old covered wagon of pioneer days along the then Old National Trail, through the railroad and interurban era and now the rapid transportation of the high-speed trains on the main line of the Pennsylvania Railroad, the bus and trucking industries on paved road 40, and in the air the regularly scheduled and beaconed route of the TWA, one of our greatest air transportation systems.

(b) Being an up-to-date agricultural and small manufacturing community, a subject bringing out these interests would prove popular, emphasis being placed on corn, hogs, wheat, cattle, dairy products and poultry, since these are the leading products.

Paragraph "(c)" discussed schools, the library, and local churches. It ends with "Politically we take the usual Hoosier interest in up-to-the-minute happenings, leaning somewhat to the conservative side." Finally he tells Hershey that "a combination of (a) and (b) would more nearly typify the community."

By late April Hershey received information about the exact color of Single G—"rather a light bay, almost a red bay, as horsemen term it . . . darker than a light sorrel, rather between a light sorrel and a brown"—as well as information about how to acquire photographs of Hampshire

hogs. By early May the color sketch was in Washington; Rowan's response on 14 May 1941 must have shocked Hershey.

[I]t is felt that there are admirable passages throughout the design but these have not been convincingly related to one another. . . . [T]he theme of travel and communications . . . were [sic] good but need not be as stressed as in the present sketch. . . . The automobile and truck could be relegated more to the background. The theme of manufacturing occupying the lower right hand corner could be eliminated and these boys could be assisting the farmer at his work.

Perhaps the most disturbing feature of the present sketch was the lack of any definite statement in back of the foreground group [Single G and his trainers]. It is as though you had hurried over this area without any definite conviction of what you wanted to convey here. An element such as a pig suckling her offsprings must be observed from life in order to carry any convictions. The mother hog in this instance just does not do anything.

Two days later the postmaster, to whom Hershey had sent a black and white photograph of the color sketch, also sent his critical comments to the artist. After claiming he was nothing more than "a common run-of-the-garden variety of country postmaster," he proceeded to make rather specific suggestions:

Would it be possible to scale down the size of the horse somewhat and give the other features of the picture correspondingly added size and importance, including as an additional link in the transportation idea, a likeness of one of our transcontinental planes which makes this route at least once each hour in [one] or the other direction.

He then added that the picture "shows all the figures in a very lifelike manner and certainly can be grasped by our citizens." He then closed with another curious commentary, this time about Thomas Hart Benton's murals from the Indiana pavilion at the Chicago World's Fair:

I had the pleasure of seeing the murals of Dr. Benton at Indiana University last Sunday and, in spite of the controversy which has raged about them, they did appeal to me, although if there ever was an artistic dumb[b]ell, I'm it. I really did enjoy them.

An artist with less perseverance might have thrown up his hands and left the whole project behind at this stage, when everybody was picking on some aspect of the design. But on 23 May Hershey tried to explain to the Section why the sketch looked as it did and what it meant by offering "an explanation concerning a few of the points of criticism." He mentioned that he had conducted "rather extensive research about the community involved," including a trip there to "gather a first-hand verification of the results."

> I cannot help feeling that if the many decorations of this kind which are being produced all over the country are to have any true significance, they should certainly attempt, at least, to express the temper of the immediate locality. The inclusion of the motor car, the truck and train . . . was not intended simply as a "theme of travel and communication," but was based on the sincere pride the citizens of Cambridge City take in the location of their town on Route 40 (the old National Highway) and the main line of the Pennsylvania Railroad. . . . I sent a photograph of the sketch [to the postmaster] and he is disturbed because I haven't carried this angle further to include the air transports that regularly pass over the "city." On that score I am quite willing to admit that enough is enough.
>
> I should be delighted to have the boys in the lower right-hand corner swinging a sulky into position for "Single G." However (and may I be forgiven my "artistic prostitution"), the boys are assembling a machine for "political reasons," a heavy metal roller manufactured in Cambridge City's largest industrial plant—one of the few large plants in the country manufacturing this kind of equipment. I personally would find little difficulty in relegating this to the traditional background position.

He then apologized for the incomplete sketch he had sent. "I am fully aware that many of the details must certainly be observed, studied and sketched from life; but it seemed to me that since a full-sized cartoon was also required, the evidence of this study would be expressed there."

Usually that level of mea culpa would have been enough to secure for an artist a kindly response from Rowan, but not so for Hershey.

> I have read your letter with the greatest interest but do not feel that your argument covers the shortcomings of the sketch submitted to this office. With all apologies I cannot understand how a serious artist can turn out even the most preliminary sketch without indication of an allegiance and respect for good drawing. . . .
>
> As to composition you have made the dynamics ever obvious. Somewhat less insistence and greater acquaintance with the actual elements of the design (thus making for conviction) will improve the composition.

On 29 July Hershey responded: "I had no intention in my previous letter of offering any 'arguments' in defense of my first sketch. I merely wished to express what I believed must have been a misunderstanding on my part."

Finally on 26 August Hershey received a grudging approval from Washington of his full-sized cartoon:

> You may proceed with the actual painting but it would be very well for you to continue to check with nature in order to give your facile drawing the stamp of conviction. Continue by all means to check the horse.
>
> I believe that you are tempted to achieve a sense of rhythm and strength by forcing cubical shapes into a kind of diagonal distortion. In my humble opinion it would be much better to create a form with less of the commercial art school stamp making simple statements about the things of this world, without the benefit of frosting.

On 19 November Hershey wrote to the postmaster, apologizing for not having kept him abreast of the changes. "I'm afraid some of the ideas we had you will find have not been carried out in the mural. Although I think it has come out very well, I have, of course, had to accede to the opinions of the Section of Fine Arts in Washington."

The mural was installed a few days later, and on 27 November 1941 Hershey wrote to the Section:

> The Postmaster, his staff and the citizens of Cambridge City who saw the decoration seemed pleased and proud to have it. I must admit to having felt no little satisfaction at having the approval of William Barefoot. He was the owner of "Single G," the horse that forms the central motif of the decoration.

By the end of 1941 commissions were becoming more and more scarce, and Samuel F. Hershey painted no other murals for the Section of Fine Arts.

TITLE
Indiana Agriculture

SIZE
16' x 5'1"

ARTIST
Frank Long

FEE
$1,000

BASIS FOR THE AWARD
*"Designs submitted in
Harrisonburg, Va. competition"*

MEDIUM
Oil on canvas

DATES
*Contract 14 March 1942 for 200
calendar days*
*Postmaster letter confirming
installation, 17 July 1942*

LOCATION OF BUILDING
300 East Main Street

For Frank Long the advent of the federal art programs meant acceptance and extended employment, beginning with the short-lived Public Works of Art Project (PWAP), 1933-34, for which he painted murals at Berea College, in Berea, Kentucky, his hometown. In 1937 he was occupied with murals in the Louisville, Kentucky, federal building under the Treasury Relief Art Project (TRAP), probably as master artist. In 1938 he completed a series of four murals for the Hagerstown, Maryland, post office under the Section, followed in 1939 by a single panel for the Morehead, Kentucky, post office lobby. He returned to his hometown, Berea, for another post office mural commissioned in 1940, before he switched his attention in 1941 to Drumright, Oklahoma, for his fourth post office mural.

Even before the Drumright mural was installed, Long sought additional contracts due to his financial needs and his draft status. He wrote Edward B. Rowan on 23 January 1942:

I don't think there is much chance of my being called for a good many months yet because I have not yet fully recovered from the superficial aspects of the recent operation, but I do feel that this factor should be considered as an urgency in making this appointment.

In his reply, Rowan explained a problem the Section faced:

> One of the reasons for the delay in inviting you [to submit sketches]
> was that I was in the hope that a similar project might be made
> available in Kentucky, but this has not materialized in view of the
> fact that the building program has been curtailed during the emer-
> gency. Artists may regard themselves very fortunate indeed that all
> of the mural reservations have not been likewise curtailed.

However, an invitation to submit sketches for Crawfordsville did
come, and the contract was written on 14 March 1942.

Of the twenty-nine artists who painted murals in Indiana post
offices, twenty-three of them received at least two commissions
throughout the United States. Around the country during the Section's
1934 to 1943 reign, twelve artists became what we might call today
"super stars," that is, they received five or six Section or TRAP commissions. Two of those artists worked in Indiana: Avery Johnson, who
painted *Autumn Fields* for Liberty, and Frank Long, who prepared
Indiana Agriculture for Crawfordsville. Incidentally, of the six artists
who received more than one commission for Indiana—Grant Christian, William A. Dolwick, Donald M. Mattison, Henrik Martin Mayer,
Jessie Hull Mayer, and Alan Tompkins—only Dolwick did not live
in Indiana.

The correspondence between Long and Rowan about the Crawfordsville mural is an indication of the way the Section had to relax its
programs and procedures with the "emergency" and the disappearance
of artists and buildings for commission. Rather than send all his
sketches to Washington for selection, Long simply sent the best on 9
March 1942 and asked for approval.

> I have made several other sketches before arriving at this concep-
> tion but since none of them compared favorably, in my estimation,
> with the present one, I have not sent them on to you. I hope, as
> usual, that if the design meets with your approval, if there are
> revisions to be made you will let me know right away.

He then goes on to "suggest" a change in contract procedures, something no artist would have dared propose only a year or two before:

> It has occurred to me in connection with this job that it might be
> possible to dispense with the two-inch scale design and substitute
> a three-quarter inch scale perspective sketch of the west wall of the
> lobby, in color and showing the mural in place. . . . I have found, in
> the past, that I sometimes lose some of the charm and spontaneity

of a first conception in carrying it through so many repetitious
restatements. I work best from a reasonably accurate drawing and
a diagrammatic indication of local color.

The foreboding of urgency that Long sensed and passed along to
Rowan in his January letter became a reality just six weeks later.

> I'm afraid that the time element on this job may prove more impor-
> tant than it has on my other commissions. I plan to volunteer for
> the army just as soon as this work is completed, but I may even be
> called before then.

Rowan okayed the speedup of the procedure and made only one design
comment in his reply: "Perhaps you will wish to check the figures in
scale in middle distance as the work progresses."

By the time Long wrote to Rowan in early July to say the mural was
finished and on the wall in Crawfordsville, the artist was connected
with "the Camouflage Section," thanks to a recommendation from
Rowan. One can almost feel in Rowan's reply a realization that the two
never again would have a professional relationship: "My only regret
relative to your work is that I have not had the opportunity to visit
your studio occasionally to discuss it with you. Please think of me
always as a friend who wishes to help you."

On 17 July 1942 the postmaster sent the official installation letter to
Washington for *Indiana Agriculture*, which proved to be the next-to-
the-last mural installed in Indiana.

Frank Long also painted *Transportation of the Mail* for Hagerstown,
Maryland, in 1938; *The Rural Free Delivery* for Morehead, Kentucky, in
1939; *Berea Commencement in the Old Days* for Berea, Kentucky, in
1940; and *Oklahoma Land Rush* for Drumright, Oklahoma, in 1941.

TITLE
From Such Beginnings Sprang the County of Lake, Indiana

SIZE
11'10" x 4'8"

ARTIST
George Melville Smith

FEE
$610

BASIS FOR THE AWARD
"Competent work executed under the Treasury Department Art Projects"

MEDIUM
Oil on canvas

DATES
Contract 25 February 1938 for 95 calendar days

Postmaster letter confirming installation, 11 October 1938

LOCATION OF BUILDING
128 South East Street

O f the thirty-seven murals originally installed in Indiana post office lobbies, only five dealt with the town's founding: Attica's *Trek of the Covered Wagons to Indiana,* Boonville's *Boonville Beginnings,* Hobart's *Early Hobart,* Ligonier's *Cutting Timber,* and Crown Point's *From Such Beginnings Sprang the County of Lake, Indiana.* This is a somewhat low percentage, especially when compared with Eastern seaboard or West Coast states, but not atypical of midwestern states where the agricultural and industrial development of the towns received greater recognition.

The work by George Melville Smith for Crown Point is the most detailed, most crowded of the five town-founding murals. While Reva Jackman and Ida Abelman brought the covered wagons into the state, Fay E. Davis portrayed the removal of the forests for farming, and William A. Dolwick provided buildings, businessmen, and two Native Americans in Hobart, George Melville Smith gave the viewers all the above items except established businessmen in his Crown Point mural. And with the group of early settlers and established farmers shown, it can be assumed that a business will be set up soon to serve those persons.

Smith, who lived in Chicago when invited on 27 October 1937 to submit designs for the Crown Point mural, was able to visit the community several times to conduct the suggested study of the locale and its inhabitants. In a 4 January 1938 letter to Edward B. Rowan, Smith told the Washington officials, "I spent considerable time in research and in visiting some interesting descendants of the pioneers in that section." Perhaps because he spent so much time conducting his research and developing his sketches, when the contract finally was written he was given only ninety-five calendar days to complete the mural, an unusually short amount of time.

A few days before the mural was installed, Smith sent a detailed description of his narrative to the Section office:

> The predominating figure on the right side of the mural typifies the man who is known as the founder of Crown Point, Indiana, namely, Solon Robinson. Born in Tolland, Connecticut, in 1803, the great-grandson of a Puritan who came with the Pilgrims, married to Mariah Evans of Philadelphia, he came first to Jennings County and then on to Lake County in 1834. His contact with the Indians was friendly and sympathetic; one, to whom he refers especially in his writings, Mewonitoc by name, is represented by the principal Indian in the group. Another of the earliest settlers was Hiram S. Bennett, who came in 1833, and another Bartlett Woods, an Englishman, came in 1837.
>
> Solon Robinson built the log house shown in the background, which house served as shelter for those newly arrived, as well as for those still on their way. The group of new arrivals on the left are being welcomed by the man, Solon Robinson, and his wife in the middle ground. The Indians, in a quandary, are contemplating moving on westward.
>
> Solon Robinson was the first Postmaster; he built the first Court house with $500 of his own money and dedicated the structure as a community building—postoffice, church, Sunday School, for elections, Temperance meetings, even serving as a jail, until 1851. He formed a Squatter's band, went with them as their leader, each taking a shotgun, and made such a speech that the speculators, who had planned to buy up the Lake County claims that had been surveyed and put up for sale at LaPorte, were denied the right to bid. The settlers then bought their lands on long time payments. Then Solon was crowned with the new name "Squatter King" and so Crown Point or King's Point became the name of the settlement.
>
> In later years he became a writer on agriculture and originated the National Agricultural Society in 1841 in Washington, D.C., with branches in several states.
>
> All the settlers united in one common cause—"To live and let live."

From that thorough description Smith might well have been qualified to serve as a historian, as well as a painter. Indeed, he began his formal art study not as a painter, but as an architect's apprentice at age fourteen, followed by evening classes at the Art Institute of Chicago at age seventeen, and then became a commercial artist "as a means of earning a livelihood, and to help support my parents." That work enabled him to spend eighteen months traveling and studying in Europe in 1925-26, including studying at Andre Lhote's school in Paris. At one time he worked with the Federal Art Project as supervisor and as "Consultant on Art."

When the mural was completed and installed, Crown Point's *Lake County Star* of 24 June 1938 commented upon Smith's portrayal of "a group of the county's first white settlers in meeting with an Indian and his Pottawattomie squaw," but never giving Mewonitoc's name in the story.

> Solon Robinson the first white settler, his wife Marie and two children, the artist says, are portrayed in the mural as the picture's background, and with them a group of pioneers who followed after Robinson and his family had blazed the trail.
>
> Yonder in the distance across a clearing, is a log cabin school house with children romping at play. At the left of the painting, done in softly shaded colors, a covered wagon drawn by a yoke of oxen is coming into view from the surrounding woodland, preceded by a woman with babe in arms astride a horse, depicting the hardships endured by motherhood in those pioneer days. . . .
>
> The artist's creative mind brought out clearly a picture of Crown Point as it was in 1834, nothing having been omitted that emphasizes the founding of the community by that little group of pioneers who followed Solon Robinson and his family into the wilderness.

George Melville Smith did another town-founding mural, *There Was a Vision*, for Elmhurst, Illinois, also in 1938. For Park Forest, Illinois, in 1940 he prepared *Indians Cede the Land*, portraying the step before the settlers could legally occupy the Indians' lands. All his murals portray historical events in American cultural history.

TITLE
The Arrival of the Mail in Culver

SIZE
10'6" x 4'6"

ARTIST
Jessie Hull Mayer

FEE
$500

BASIS FOR THE AWARD
*Won second place in Lafayette
competition*

MEDIUM
Oil on canvas

DATES
*Contract 25 May 1937 for
270 calendar days*

*Postmaster letter confirming
installation, 7 March 1938*

LOCATION OF BUILDING
115 West Jefferson Street

In 1938, with the installation of her mural in Culver, Jessie Hull Mayer began a one-post-office-mural-per-year schedule that lasted through 1941, an enviable record by any standard.

Her first invitation to submit sketches came as the result of placing second in the design competition in 1936 for the Lafayette post office, a competition won by her husband Henrik Martin Mayer. Late in 1936 Edward B. Rowan wrote to her asking if she and Henrik were related since they lived at the same address. In what today we might view as a sign of the times, Jessie responded on 5 October: "Although I regret not winning this job myself, it is perhaps better for the peace of our family that you did not award it to me, because I am Mrs. Henrik Martin Mayer."

The official letter from the Section inviting Jessie to submit designs for Culver was sent on 30 December 1936, and on 8 January 1937 she wrote back to Washington: "The invitation of the Section of Painting and Sculpture to submit designs . . . was the first mail I received in 1937, and will keep me cheered up for the whole year."

The approved project is unique in the Indiana panoply of murals, for this is the only mural with a central panel flanked by six side panels with related but singular designs. Rather than trying to cram one panel with all the elements important to and appropriate to the Culver area, Mayer chose to show the unity of the major constituents: the townspeople, the farmers, and the military academy in the middle panel, with the ancillary activities in the side panels. Interestingly enough, however, the Section had little commentary on the side panels except to suggest once that the color of the central panel could be enlivened "by the introduction of some of the reds used in the outer panels."

In a 13 May letter Rowan did suggest that "it would be a courtesy if you would present your design to the Postmaster in Culver for his comments although the design has been approved in this office." This little aside comment focuses on a continuing concern faced by the artists, the Section (and indirectly the staff of the Procurement Division of the Treasury), and the local postmasters: who had the final say over the content and/or acceptability of a painting?

At times in the history of the Section, the onus seemed to be upon the artist to gain approval of the postmaster for the designs before they were submitted to Washington, while at other times, such as is the case here, the Section seemed to be saying that the design had been approved, regardless of what the postmaster might have to say. The Section's *Bulletin* in 1939 carried a reprint of an editorial from the *Washington Post* about this same concern:

> There can be very little doubt that [the Section], through its practice of awarding contracts on the basis of anonymous competition, has been responsible for a great surge of artistic energy in the Nation. It is not merely that it has uncovered American talents in unexpected abundance, and that the work submitted has shown an extraordinary imaginative vitality. The real significance lies in the fact that introduction of these murals into thousands of small post offices is kindling an aesthetic awareness in millions of Americans, just as, centuries ago, it was kindled in Italian peasants by the introduction of pieta and other paintings into village churches. . . .
>
> This leads us to the question of whether the national taste is a proper concern of a democratic government. One answer is that great art is as important a form of wealth as great industries. If industry is dependent upon the existence of markets, art is dependent upon the existence of taste. The same logic which permits a government to protect national industries by tariffs or trade treaties might easily justify the development of a national art by appropriate and effective means.

When the newspaper article appeared at the time of the mural's installation, no one seemed to question the appropriateness of the design. Virginia Moorhead Mannon, writing in the 19 February 1938 edition of the *Indianapolis Times,* began her commentary on Culver with a reflection upon the mural as part of the decor.

> When the inhabitants of Culver and its environs saunter into their neat little postoffice today they'll find a startling change in the hitherto blank wall space of the postmaster's door. Adding considerably to the Federal decor is a colorful mural depicting "The Arrival of the Mail," the work of Mrs. Henrik Mayer, young Indianapolis artist. Mrs. Mayer, who was commissioned to do the painting as a U. S. Treasury Department art project, rolled up the canvas and took it by truck to Culver yesterday.

Mannon then switched to the standard explication provided by a Section press release:

> The mural, which is 10½ feet long and 4½ feet high, consists of a large center panel with smaller panels at either end. The center figures, two-thirds life size, include two cadets reading letters, two postal employees bending over the mail bags and a farmer and summer resident calling for mail. Six smaller studies picturing activities around the lake—agriculture, camping, swimming, Culver Military Academy, sailing and riding—are represented in the narrow side panels.
>
> The coloring of the canvas is designed to blend with the cream-colored wall, the pinky-gray marble wainscoting and dark brown woodwork of the postoffice interior. The warm gray running through the study harmonizes with the blue-gray of the mailmen's attire and the absolute gray of the cadet uniforms. . . .
>
> "The Arrival of the Mail" is the first mural painted by the young artist, who received her B.F.A. at Yale in 1932. It represents a year's work with steady painting from 10 a.m. to 5 p.m. daily during the past two months.

Jessie Hull Mayer completed murals for Jasper, *Indiana Farming Scene in Late Autumn,* in 1939, for Canton, Missouri, *Winter Landscape,* in 1940, and for Lagrange, Indiana, *The Corn School,* in 1941.

TITLE
*Filling the Water Jugs
Haymaking Time*

SIZE
11′8″ x 3′10″

ARTIST
Gail W. Martin

FEE
$560

BASIS FOR THE AWARD
*"The merit of the design
submitted in the Interior
Department competition"*

MEDIUM
Oil on canvas

DATES
*Contract 15 December 1938 for
259 calendar days*

*Postmaster letter confirming
installation, 17 October 1939*

LOCATION OF BUILDING
101 West Marion Street

Whether it can be called luck or serendipity or whatever, sometimes an artist, a locale, and a subject
all come together to produce much more than the
sum of their separate parts would seem to indicate
before the work began.

Such good fortune occurred in Danville when Gail W. Martin was
invited on 25 August 1938 to submit sketches for a mural in the post
office lobby. The end of August is harvesttime on the farms around
Danville, and Martin probably made a trip to the country with a special eye to the potential for design elements. But it was not until 8
December that Martin sent sketches to Washington. His letter to
Edward B. Rowan expressed both his preferred designs and the reason
for his preference:

> The first of these sketches is of a group around the public drinking
> fountain in Danville, but they are not very successful as they now
> stand and I have not worked with them to any length.
>
> The second design is a group of farmers around the pump getting
> a drink and filling their water jugs during hay-making time. Of this
> there are a few crude sketches and one fairly complete study in

black and white, mounted on the one inch scale of the lobby wall. This subject, of course, is my preference of this bunch of sketches. . . .

I have had considerable delay in getting these sketches to you, this delay was mostly because of a job I was working on that had to be finished. Now, however, I have my own studio and am quite anxious to do the color study and the cartoon and get to the actual painting.

I feel that this subject is well suited to the locale of Danville, for it is definitely a farming town like so many of the other small towns in this part of the country.

In my youth I lived on a farm and now visit frequently the farm of my wife's parents just outside Franklin, Indiana. Hence, I am quite sympathetic to, and feel that I have more than a passing knowledge of, farm life.

With that personal endorsement of the appropriateness of the rural design to the locale and the indication of the artist's preference, how could the Section, in all good faith, have chosen any sketch other than the water jug sketch?

One small problem artists occasionally faced shows itself in Martin's proposal to the Section, that is, where and how to locate the mural on the wall relative to other objects such as bulletin boards, door frames, etc. Apparently Martin's sketch that showed the mural on the wall had the edges of the mural stretching across the entire area above the postmaster's door, several inches beyond the edges of the bulletin boards immediately below where the mural would be. Rowan suggested a change:

Relative to the dimensions of the finished work we have found that a mural becomes more architectural in a space of this nature if the ends of the mural coincide with the outer edge of the bulletin boards, which would cut down your space a little more. I would like you to consider this as a possibility, allowing the wall color to go up on the sides of the wall.

One other concern about canvas size and placement also occurred in the Danville mural, that is, should the canvas stop at the top of the door frame or go below it another ten to twelve inches? The Washington office was concerned because of the little boy who sits just to the left of center in the foreground, filling one of the jugs. In Martin's original sketch the boy stood at that location, but only the top half of his body was portrayed, and the Washington office had a particular

dislike for partial bodies in mural designs. Rowan suggested either that the figure of the boy be moved up into the center so that the entire body would show or that the canvas be extended down the side of the door enough to show the entire body. The artist did neither, but solved the problem by having the boy sit on the wellhead beside the pump, thereby leaving enough room to show the whole body without extending the canvas or moving the figure.

Finally Martin completed his mural, a "simple but vital design" in the best sense of that phrase, showing five persons filling up water jugs or getting a drink of cool water from the tub which the central figure fills with the pump. This event took place hundreds, if not thousands, of times every year on farms across the land, so why did Martin choose to aggrandize this particular moment, giving the viewer, even today, an almost photographic "slice of life"? Only he could tell us that, but certainly the audience for whom he prepared this mural responded in a unanimously approving way.

About a month after the mural was installed, Bertha Higgins, the postmistress, sent the official letter to Washington confirming the satisfactory installation and apologizing for being late in the dispatch of the letter.

We people in Danville and in Hendricks County realize we have in this office a very beautiful and also a very interesting mural.

Strangers who have come into the office, many times have come to my door to express their admiration for this work and ask who did it.

One other thing that appeals to me is—this is a strictly farming district so of course, Mr. Martin's selection is the most appropriate picture he could have painted for us.

We are more than pleased with Mr. Martin's work.

That same day she wrote to Martin:

I wish that you might slip in some day to hear the admirable things the people say about your work.

Men, women, and children linger to talk about it and even old men and women have heard about the new picture in the Post Office and have come in to see it.

We are grateful to you and the [post office] department.

Even an anonymous local newspaper writer said of the mural: "It is a typical Hoosier scene with natural figures rather than the grotesque figures so commonly depicted in modern murals."

Gail W. Martin did no other Section murals.

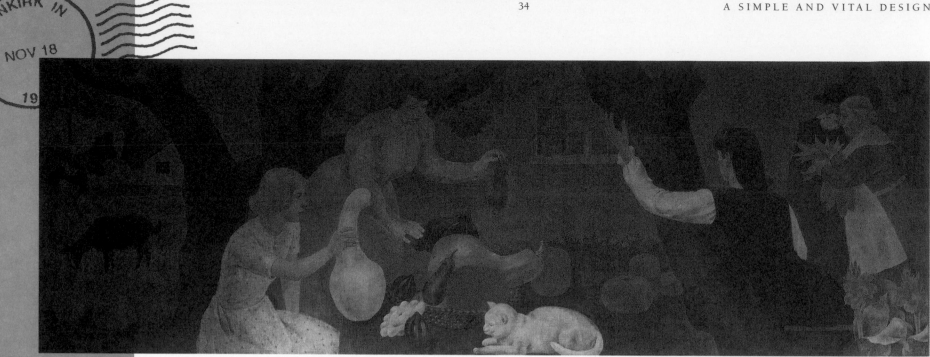

TITLE
*Preparations for Autumn Festival,
Dunkirk*

SIZE
13'7" x 4'6"

ARTIST
Frances Foy

FEE
$650

BASIS FOR THE AWARD
*"On the basis of competent
designs submitted in St. Louis
competition"*

MEDIUM
Oil on canvas

DATES
*Contract 18 November 1940 for
117 calendar days*

*Postmaster letter confirming
installation, 13 March 1941*

LOCATION OF BUILDING
123 West Commerce Street

The Dunkirk mural is the fourth of five which Foy did for the Section between 1938 and 1943. This particular commission came only because the person to whom it was originally offered, Antol Shulkin, delayed so long in preparing sketches and complained so frequently about Dunkirk being too far from New York City that the Section gave him another opportunity, Canajoharie, New York.

Foy, who lived in Chicago at the time of the commission, was able to visit Dunkirk without great expense and did so, seeking information for a design, but not necessarily the usual "town-founding" or "industrial development" version of progress idea. Rather this mural and at least two of her other designs are based upon happenstance as much as upon research.

For example, when invited to submit sketches for a small mural in East Alton, Illinois, Foy visited the town to make some sketches that might prove useful at a later date. She told the Section staff there was nothing outstanding about the design for *The Letter,* just two old ladies talking about a letter "unless I tell you how I came upon the original two old ladies."

I had just been sitting in a parked car, sketching some buildings on a hill, with a homey cottage—sunflowers, fruit trees—in the immediate foreground, when a wiry old woman came out of the cottage and stood leaning on her gate. All at once her tired, troubled expression changed to a warm smile as a plump, jovial neighbor came by, holding a huge rhubarb stalk, with which she gesticulated from time to time. Immediately I began making rapid pen sketches—of hands, facial expressions, etc.—as one does when one can do so unobserved. Realizing how easily a rhubarb stalk might be transformed into a letter, and how easily this slight change would condense the whole into a uniquely dramatic moment, I decided to use these sketches as data for my mural.

Perhaps it was just a matter of being in the right place at the right time, but to recognize this common, everyday occurrence as having the potential for a "dramatic moment" requires an artistic sensitivity. For her 1943 West Allis, Wisconsin, mural she did not choose to glorify the original Native American inhabitants, the settlers, or the manufacturing, which in this Milwaukee suburb flourished again in 1943 with the advent of World War II. Instead, she prepared two large panels of *Wisconsin Wild Flowers—Spring* and *Wisconsin Wild Flowers—Autumn.* Even when she did do a more "traditional" mural, *The Advent of the Pioneer,* for a Chicago postal station, it portrayed a steam engine, the "Pioneer," at a less than dramatic moment.

My mural does not represent the first trip of the train with the excitement of celebration, but rather several years later when it had become a customary mode of travelling, and shows groups of people of that period standing about waiting for freight to be loaded onto the waiting train. The engineer is the heroic-looking man in shirt-sleeves being admired by the little girl.

With that kind of subtle awareness of the passing scene, the contemporary viewer should not be surprised that the inspiration for the Dunkirk mural was squashes.

This mural is a combination of things that especially impressed me on the trip to Dunkirk last fall. I remember goats there, and apple trees with apples still on, and the Dunkirk glass-factory chimney, and yellow corn hung up to dry. And what took my fancy most were these huge, goose-neck squashes, like gorgeous musical instruments. They are hardly natural looking.

With the Dunkirk invitation, Foy, as always, had submitted several sketches for consideration by the Section. Edward B. Rowan was taken by the festival sketch, calling it "most appealing and unusual," indicating, too, that even Washington occasionally sought something other than the standard "local-scene-glorification" design.

Before Dunkirk, Frances Foy had completed *The Letter* in East Alton, Illinois, in 1936; *Advent of the Pioneer* in Chicago in 1938; and *Hiawatha Returning with Minnehaha* for Gibson City, Illinois, in 1940. After the Dunkirk mural she did the two large panels in West Allis, *Wisconsin Wild Flowers—Spring* and *Wisconsin Wild Flowers—Autumn,* in 1943.

TITLE
Local Industry

SIZE
14'6" x 6'

ARTIST
Jean Swiggett

FEE
$650

BASIS FOR THE AWARD
"As a result of competent designs submitted in Jasper, Indiana, competition"

MEDIUM
Oil on canvas

DATES
Contract 15 July 1939 for 200 calendar days
Postmaster letter confirming installation, 3 April 1940

LOCATION OF BUILDING
1265 North Main Street

When Jean Swiggett of Long Beach, California, entered the regional competition for the Jasper post office mural, he did not realize he had three surprises in store. First, he did not win the Jasper competition, but he did come in as runner-up, meaning he would be invited to submit sketches for a mural in a different location, which was the second surprise; the invitation came for the building in Franklin. Swiggett was born and reared in Franklin; because of that "attachment" he, a California resident, had been allowed to enter the Jasper competition in the first place.

Even though the invitation letter came on 17 January 1939, he did not respond with any drawings until June because he was involved in "painting quite a large mural in egg tempera under the Federal Art project" in Redondo Beach, California. He had been hired by Paul Sample to work with him on a large, three-panel mural for the Treasury Relief Art Project (TRAP). Swiggett worked as the assistant, filling in outlines created by Sample, attaching canvas, and mixing oils for Sample, the master artist. Because Swiggett, who qualified for relief assistance at the time, had been told he would lose his relief qualification once he received a contract and payment from the Section, he decided to stall on the Franklin job until finished with Redondo Beach in June. He probably had justification for his concern, for although he would not be paid even part of his commission until certain contractual details had been completed, in theory, at least, he was employed and was not eligible for TRAP assistance. Earlier Swiggett had held a similar position as assistant to Norman Chamberlain in another TRAP undertaking in Huntington Beach, California. Here Chamberlain designed just the main panel of the seven panels covering all the walls from wainscot to ceiling, while Swiggett and Ivan Bartlett designed the others. The latter experience certainly provided more training than the former, but Swiggett was happy to take any art work available.

The artist's third surprise came when he submitted the designs for Franklin. He did not have to travel back to his hometown for inspiration or did he have to draw upon his memories for appropriate design elements. He reworked the Jasper design "with only a few details changed to make the mural fit the Franklin location." Even the Washington office seemed happy with what it saw, according to a 15 September 1939 letter from Edward B. Rowan:

> The only suggestion offered is that the subject matter is limited exclusively to the activities of men and you may wish to introduce some female figures, particularly in the Agriculture theme as the work progresses in the full size cartoon.

As the mural shows, Swiggett did introduce the figure of a young girl in the lower left side of the design.

What he has put together is a fascinating dichotomy of agriculture and industry, with almost mirrorlike images symmetrically poised on the outer thirds of the panel. On the left a tall farmer with cornstalk in hand and a boy holding a calf are echoed on the right with another tall man holding a board and a boy holding a bag of some product. Behind these foreground figures appropriate buildings and other figures fill the middle ground and background. Filling the central third of the panel is what the artist said brought unity to the two groups, the post office and the railroad, both providing needed services to all elements of the community. In order to make the design location specific, Swiggett used the actual Franklin post office building as the model for the building in the painting.

About 1980 the United States Postal Service moved into new quarters at 1265 North Main Street, away from the downtown location of

the post office building depicted in Swiggett's mural. The former post office building became the city hall.

Swiggett's mural was moved into the new facility, but it was not attached to the wall. Rather it is held in a raw, unpainted frame with no backing and has been placed in an out-of-the-way location just off the main lobby. With the current inadequate lighting it cannot be enjoyed today in the way it once was, and *Local Industry* is now in the shadows.

Jean Swiggett painted no other murals for the Section.

GARRETT IN
JAN 24
1938

A SIMPLE AND VITAL DESIGN

Clearing the Right of Way

12′4″ x 5′

Joe Cox

$530

BASIS FOR THE AWARD
*"The merit of the design
submitted by you in competition"*

Oil on canvas

*Contract 24 January 1938 for
217 calendar days*
*Postmaster letter confirming
installation, 7 June 1938*

LOCATION OF THE
BUILDING
115 West Keyser Street

Within a few months of completing his degree at the John Herron Art Institute in Indianapolis, Joe Cox received a commission for the Garrett mural and a job as instructor of painting at the University of Iowa. While at Herron, Cox studied with contemporary artists Donald M. Mattison and Henrik Martin Mayer, as well as established luminaries such as Elmer Taflinger and Elliot O'Hara.

Cox's abilities were further recognized by the invitation letter from Edward B. Rowan, who, while he asked for sketches with "subject matter which embodies some idea appropriate to the building or to the particular locale of Garrett, Indiana," also praised Cox for his runner-up design in competition, the design which led to the Garrett invitation. Although the correspondence file is vague, apparently Rowan referred to Cox's submission for the San Antonio competition, a national competition, for Cox replied to the letter: "Thanks for the compliment on the San Antonio job. I am certain I can do as well or better for Garrett." If it were indeed the San Antonio competition, which drew 185 entries, which allowed Cox to achieve an "honorable mention" or other runner-up recognition, it speaks for the high quality of the artist's work. In addition, to be hired right out of art school as an instructor in the same program where Grant Wood was heading a series of mural creations for the university's library also speaks to Cox's abilities.

When he visited Garrett the artist soon found the major employer was the Baltimore and Ohio Railroad; in fact, the B & O had established the town in 1871 as a regional headquarters.

I visited Garrett to gather material, and found that it was built by the B & O Railroad. Most of the people in Garrett are interested in, or connected with, the railroad in some way.

Therefore my two most successful designs deal with the building of the railroad that is responsible for the existence of Garrett.

In this vicinity, there were a great many trestles built which were considered quite remarkable. In one of my designs I have shown this.

To call the building of the trestles "remarkable" really is an understatement, for more than three hundred trestles were constructed by the railroad crews over surrounding marshes and streams. It is this activity that the Section chose, calling the design depicting the erecting of a major trestle "unusual," but expressing confidence "it will make a wholly entertaining decoration." The train engine dominates the composition as it thrusts forward from the right hand side of the painting. Or, if one accepts that side as east—as in cartographic methodology where the top of a map is designated north, the bottom is south, the right is east, and the left is west—the engine comes barreling out from Baltimore and locations in Ohio. The design also is interesting in its use of two strong linear focal points, the train on the rails at the top and the line of logs at the bottom; both prongs point to the trestle under fabrication at the left side of the painting.

The final test of the success of a post office lobby mural was the response by the citizens of the town, so when Rowan wrote to the Garrett postmaster on 27 May 1938 asking for confirmation of the satisfactory installation of the canvas, he also asked for copies of any newspaper articles or tidbits of conversation overheard about the mural.

Have been a little slow in answering yours of May 27th . . . relative to the installation of mural in lobby of our post-office as I was anxious to find out just how our community felt about it. Am very happy to report that we have been receiving some mighty fine compliments, in fact, heard but one criticism and that of a minor nature.

Am enclosing a small clipping from the local paper and while it does not seem to be outstanding, yet, judging by the number of people coming in just to look at the mural, it must have given us more publicity than we thought.

Feel that Mr. Cox has given us a fine job, in workmanship and installation, and want to add that it is a real addition to the decoration of the building.

Joe Cox painted one other mural for the Section of Fine Arts, *Harvest,* for Alma, Michigan, in 1940.

TITLE
Gas City in Boom Days

SIZE
12'8" x 3'6"

ARTIST
William A. Dolwick

FEE
$670

BASIS FOR THE AWARD
Designs submitted in Barnesville, Ohio, competition

MEDIUM
Oil on canvas

DATES
Contract 4 January 1939 for 223 calendar days

Postmaster letter confirming installation, 28 July 1939

LOCATION OF BUILDING
123 North Second Street

William A. Dolwick's Gas City mural probably contains more architectural and material culture artifacts than any other mural in the state. From the beginning the artist intended to fill the space with reminders of the early days of the city, of the "boom days" in the late 1800s when natural gas flowed so abundantly that city officials gave it away to local manufacturing plants just as a way to entice them to locate in Gas City. About two months after he received the invitation to submit sketches for a mural, Dolwick sent one possibility to Edward B. Rowan in Washington:

> In this sketch, as suggested, I have used material peculiar to the locale of Gas City. The time is 1893, soon after the gas boom started, and the sketch shows part of the bank building, which has quite unusual architecture, the Mississinewa Hotel, the first Post Office with the original Postmaster in the doorway, typical block of stores, covered bridge, the Mississinewa River flowing on the side and back of the town, and a background of factories and gas well derricks.

Sometimes having one's abilities known by the Section could be an asset, such as when another invitation letter was sent about a new job, but at other times such knowledge led to higher expectations. After receiving the correspondence cited above, Rowan indicated his displeasure:

> I do not want this letter . . . to discourage you in any way. Frankly if we were not aware of your versatile ability I would recommend

the approval of this sketch off hand. Before doing so, however, I want you to turn the problem over in your mind for several days and submit either further proposals incorporating similar subject matter but treated with a little more imagination or entirely new subject matter. . . . You have obviously put a lot of time and thought in this work and I do want you to know that we are aware of this.

Although the original sketches are no longer available in the National Archives, on the basis of the finished mural Dolwick did not make any radical changes, at least not in terms of new subject matter, although the treatment may have varied from the original proposal.

The next sketch sent by the artist to Washington brought further negative criticism.

[T]here is a general feeling of monotony of mass throughout the design. It seems heavy to a degree and anything you can do to lighten the mood of the design will be to its advantage. These criticisms might not be justified in the color sketch with which you may now proceed.

And, indeed, Dolwick solved many of the problems by the effective use of color in the finished mural, color that allows for separation and "lightening" of the essence of the work, which, however, still contains bank, post office, covered bridge, glass factory, and the first postmaster making a delivery on his bicycle "to a River Road resident who has come to town," according to Dolwick's narrative.

Dolwick's troubles were not over, however, when the color sketch convinced the Section he should proceed with the work. He still had to hang the mural—usually a simple enough task—and had to satisfy the local "art critic," frequently a very difficult task, especially when that critic says "we'll admit that our ability as an art critic is nil . . . but. . . ."

On 20 July 1939 Dolwick wrote Rowan about the trouble he had in installing the mural, even though he had written the postmaster that the work would be done over the weekend, "thinking this would cause the least inconvenience" and disruption of official business.

However, when I arrived in town I found him quite uncooperative. He allowed me a limited time to work and apparently considered the installation an inconvenience. . . . I suppose you will understand that it leaves one with a let-down feeling.

Yet a few days later the postmaster wrote Rowan: "Installation of the mural was done in a very satisfactory way and with no inconvenience to the patrons during work hours." He also added that "public comments . . . are very complimentary with the exception of the Gas City Journal."

The editorial writer for the 28 July 1939 issue of the *Gas City Journal* is the one who disallowed himself any artistic ability, but

After two or three months of anxious waiting, since the artist was here to get ideas for a mural painting to be hung in the new Gas City postoffice, our curiosity was appeased last week when the painting arrived and was put up on the south wall of the building. . . .

We'll admit that our ability as an art critic is nil, and therefore our opinion doesn't amount to much, but the mural fails to come up to our expectations in several respects. Maybe we don't understand art and murals. Perhaps we fail to use our imagination.

Anyway, the painting assumes to depict the early history of Gas City, and some of it can be reorganized [recognized?]. There are reproductions of the bank building, and the hotel building, right enough, and a picture of the rear of the first postoffice building. The first postoffice is perched in the middle of Main and Third streets, and looks more like one of those small structures familiar in years past on the back of nearly every lot, before sanitary sewers came into use in Gas City. . . .

[The first postmaster] has dismounted from his bicycle, and is handing a letter to another man, seated in a horse and buggy. We don't know who this man is. He must be getting a special delivery letter, for no other mail was delivered at that time. . . .

The painting as a whole is a hodge-podge of vague ideas, put together without any relation to actual locations. But that seems to be a habit with murals. If you like that kind of art, the picture is all right, but we will admit that it doesn't appeal to us. Anyway the thing is there and will probably remain, whether we like it or not.

As we said before, we sadly lack imagination, and appreciation of art. So just forget it.

Luckily the postmaster also included other clippings from other papers where another anonymous critic, who also was "not an authority" on art "thought it was very attractive." A third writer pointed out the "impressionistic" mixture of views of the bank, hotel buildings, oil derricks, glass factories, the river, and a steamboat "in a rather confused fashion."

William A. Dolwick also painted *Early Hobart* for Hobart in 1938.

TITLE
Early Hobart

SIZE
12' x 5'

ARTIST
William A. Dolwick

FEE
$580

BASIS FOR THE AWARD
"Work done under the Treasury Department Art Projects"

MEDIUM
Oil on canvas

DATES
Contract 1 March 1938 for 122 calendar days

Postmaster letter confirming installation, 1 August 1938

LOCATION OF BUILDING
221 Main Street

On 28 July 1938 William A. Dolwick sent a biographical sketch to Forbes Watson, adviser in the Section of Painting and Sculpture. Watson, who was charged with gathering material to be used in press releases, had contacted Dolwick because the artist had just completed a mural for the Hobart post office lobby. Dolwick apologized for being delinquent in responding to Watson's request, but told him "the necessity of making a living has had me so tied up, that I was unable to find time to prepare the short account you asked for."

Upon graduation [from the Cleveland School of Art] I was awarded the Gottwald Traveling Fellowship for a year's study abroad. I spent one term at the Slade School, and 6 months at the Academies "Scandinav" and "Colarossi" in Paris. . . .

In 1933 I was employed under P.W.A.P., and painted two works, one an easel picture titled "A French Scene," the other a mural of Early Cleveland which is installed in the Carnegie-Lorain Branch Library of Cleveland. For four months in 1935 I painted in a C.C.C. camp located on the Oregon coast. While there I did three murals depicting camp life which were allocated to the Department of the Interior, Washington.

Four days after Edward B. Rowan sent Dolwick the standard "invitation to prepare sketches" letter about the Hobart post office, the Section official sent a personalized letter "to advise . . . relative to the type of decoration" the Washington office sought.

> I would like to call your attention to a very interesting painting of a French street scene which you did under the P.W.A.P. It is this type of approach which we would like to have you use in dealing with a subject related to Indiana or Hobart, in particular.

Although no record of that French street scene remains, the impression was strong enough on Rowan for him to specifically ask for a similar proposal for Hobart, and, since the correspondence files do not contain references to changing the style of the proposals to match the easel painting, a contemporary viewer can assume fairly safely that the easel painting style is similar to that found in Hobart's mural.

For many years Hobart has had an active historical society, and Dolwick was the beneficiary of that energy for he related in another letter, presumably again to Forbes Watson, "all the buildings represented are authentic in detail [having worked] from old photographs" owned by local residents. Additional information also came from "a Mrs. Floyd E. Demmon, who is compiling a history of this section under the Writers project set-up."

> The building on the extreme left side of the painting is the trading post, general store and Post Office. Part of the interior is shown, with pigeon-hole letter file, and the figure of an Indian trading furs for supplies from the store-keeper. The building directly behind this is the Art Gallery, which was built by the founder of the town whose avocation was painting, and who had amassed quite a collection of canvases. The next structure to the right is the blacksmith shop, towards which the blacksmith, who is reading a letter, is walking.

> The large building right is the grist mill, which was powered by water from the river. Along the side of the mill is shown a wagon being loaded with sacks of flour. At the extreme right of the composition is shown the saw mill.

> The three foreground figures are representative of city fathers. They are not genuine portraits, but are modified for pictorial purposes.

After the artwork was cemented to the wall, Rowan wrote to Dolwick, congratulating him on "the high quality" of the work:

> It is a neat looking job, well painted and one of which you may be justly proud. The types which you used are particularly commendable.

> The only criticism which one might offer is that the lower extremities of the Indian sitting on the front porch do not seem completely realized. In other words his lower extremities seemed crowded. But this is a minor detail which will occur only to a few of the many people who enjoy the mural.

According to *Along the Route: A History of Hobart, Indiana, Post Offices and Postmasters,* a 1979 publication of the Hobart Historical Society, the mural almost was destroyed.

> By 1966 the painting had become dingy and deteriorated. It was scheduled to be discarded when remodeling began in 1965. Postmaster H. Emden Rippe thought it should be preserved and local artist Victor Sable beautifully restored the mural.

William A. Dolwick also painted a 1939 mural for Gas City, *Gas City in Boom Days*.

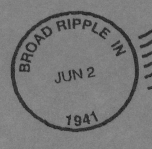

TITLE
Suburban Street

SIZE
11'9" x 5'2"

ARTIST
Alan Tompkins

FEE
$860

BASIS FOR THE AWARD
Designs submitted for the St. Louis, Missouri, competition

DATES
Contract 2 June 1941 for 181 calendar days; changed later to 302 days; extended for 60 days

Postmaster letter confirming installation never received; Tompkins's letter of installation, 29 May 1942

LOCATION OF BUILDING
6255 Carrollton Avenue

The Broad Ripple commission was the third Indiana commission for Alan Tompkins. This commission was preceded by Martinsville in 1937 and North Manchester in 1938. Only one other muralist, Jessie Hull Mayer, received three commissions for Indiana locations. Tompkins's Broad Ripple mural also was the first in the trio of works completed in 1942 that ended the Section's painting program in Indiana, being followed by Frank Long's Crawfordsville work in July and Marguerite Zorach's Monticello mural in November.

The last paragraph of Tompkins's description of his Martinsville mural applies equally well to his Broad Ripple effort: "In general I have tried to convey a sense of the warmth and genuineness of friendly interest in others in American community life." If that feeling inspired his Broad Ripple mural, it might explain some of the difficulties he had in completing the design to the satisfaction of the Section. While Tompkins had concluded his earlier works with only occasional suggestions from the Washington office about placement of figures or the color scheme to be used in those canvases, from the beginning of the

Broad Ripple mural there seemed to be a clash between the artist's efforts and the interpretation of those efforts by the Section staff.

Although officially invited to submit sketches for this location on 7 February 1941 it was not until 28 April that Tompkins sent two pencil drawings for consideration.

> I feel the [smaller] one titled "Having wonderful time. Wish you were here" is the more original idea and will gain most by the use of whimsically brilliant color.
>
> The community served by the Post office is entirely residential and contains many fine homes. . . . No historical nor industrial subjects would be at all appropriate here. The lobby is very light and will require a high-keyed, colorful type of decoration.

The Section staff agreed the small sketch was humorous but felt it would be "forced" when taken to a large scale, so they instructed Tompkins to develop a color sketch of his suburban street scene.

That sketch brought strong negative criticism from Edward B. Rowan: "The relationship of the walls adjoining the sidewalk and the red brick building in back of it is unexplained. . . . What is the large green area? . . . Numerous details are confused." Tompkins admitted the concerns were legitimate but argued with their intent:

> Throughout I feel that your criticism attempts to fit my sketch into the [Aaron] Bohrod or [Reginald] Marsh type of realistic genre, whereas I was, frankly, trying to come nearer to the flatness and monumentality of Giotto (the perspectives of whose backgrounds would hardly survive the criticism you applied to mine). . . .
>
> I should have known better! My abilities simply do not lie in the direction of effective stylization, and the rather brittle naturalism which I achieved in its stead fitted poorly against the background and seemed to demand that the whole thing be "explainable."

By October he had completed a new color sketch with even more changes: "I feel sure you will agree the new effort is more lyrical and much more worth while enlarging." In order to make these changes and convert them into an approvable cartoon, however, Tompkins asked for an extension on his contract, noting that "a mere adherence to the stated terms of the [original] contract would certainly have been the easier course for me. I have chosen a course which I felt sure would be more acceptable in the long run to all parties concerned, especially to those who will use the Post Office and see the mural frequently." The extension was granted, even though by this time in 1941 the Section and the other federal art programs received increasing pressure from many sides in government and outside government to curtail their activities.

The new color sketch, however, failed to satisfy Rowan, whose 8 November 1941 letter to the artist was negative, again.

> I regret to inform you that the latest one is not as satisfactory as the previous one. The forced art forms used in the drawing carry no sincerity and conviction for us and we are confident would not be as acceptable to the people of Indiana as the previous sketch.

Tompkins did as he was told and developed the cartoon from the first revised sketch.

This time Rowan's letter, dated 24 January 1942, brought good news. This cartoon "may not be as arty in approach but it certainly carries a sincerity and an appeal that the preliminary sketches lacked. There is conviction in your scene which, in my humble opinion, is very worthy."

From this date until several letters in May and June the correspondence is slight, probably because the staff of the Washington office diminished in size as the activities of the Section lessened since fewer buildings were available for decoration and because Washington was engaged in wartime operations with little time for art and other cultural affairs.

A similar sense of urgency and motivation may have affected Tompkins as he worked on the cartoon in November and December of 1941, that is, just before and just after Pearl Harbor. As he painted in early 1942 apparently he felt compelled to try to depict American values in his canvas, values fundamental to our way of life which would justify his employment. As he said in a 1978 interview: "Getting the commission from the government had a kind of reassurance to it that it was a commission from the people of the country, so to speak."

In a letter to Rowan on 5 May, after the canvas was completed and just shortly before it was cemented to the lobby wall in Broad Ripple, Tompkins described the subject matter:

> The mural is an attempt to interpret in visual terms those intangibles of democratic community life which we are now fighting to preserve.
>
> It represents children and grownups taking advantage of a glowing Spring morning for promenading, chatting, cycling, shopping, and receiving their mail. But the real subject is the atmosphere of mutual trust and friendliness, of peace and security, that is the essence of life in a democracy.

Rowan liked that wording so much that he must have used it in the official press release when the mural was installed, for most of Tompkins's words appear in the *Indianapolis Sunday Star* on 28 June 1942.

The final correspondence between Tompkins and the Section came when the artist wrote to request the last payment due him for his canvas, which normally would have been authorized following receipt of a letter from the postmaster stating the mural had, indeed, been installed satisfactorily. The Broad Ripple postmaster never sent such confirmation, even after repeated requests from Rowan's office. Finally, when Tompkins wrote in November that he was about to enlist in the army and wanted to "get his affairs in order," including this payment, Rowan authorized the compensation.

Alan Tompkins also painted *The Arrival of the Mail* for Martinsville in 1937; *Indiana Farm—Sunday Afternoon* for North Manchester in 1938; and *Daniel Boone on a Hunting Trip in Watauga County* for Boone, North Carolina, in 1940.

In July 1935 President Franklin D. Roosevelt earmarked $530,784 to the director of procurement of the Treasury for the Treasury Relief Art Project (TRAP), a special relief program to provide assistance to educational, professional, and clerical persons. In December 1938 the program was discontinued "because it was administratively determined by Treasury officials that it would be better policy for [it] not to be engaged in this work on account of the relief requirements. It was deemed that such employment by the Department was a duplication of the activities of the Works Progress Administration."

During that three and one-half years of operation, TRAP received almost $850,000 to hire master artists and mural assistants for mural painting, easel painters, carpenters, wood carvers, and other craftspersons. The money also provided them with paint, canvas, tools, and other items needed to help them do their jobs. Originally 90 percent of the persons hired were supposed to be on relief or, if they did not technically qualify for the official relief rolls, be indigent. Ultimately that stipulation had to be modified to a 75 percent indigent, 25 percent nonindigent ratio in order to hire enough qualified master artists.

Whereas the funding for the projects of the Section of Fine Arts came from construction costs of new buildings, TRAP funds could go

TITLE
Mail—Transportation and Delivery and Early and Present Day Indianapolis Life

SIZE
7 vertical panels, approx. 4' x 10'

ARTIST
Grant Christian, master artist Reynolds Selfridge, assistant

FEE
$186 per month $93 per month

BASIS OF THE AWARD
Designs submitted in competition

MEDIUM
Oil on canvas

DATES
16 September 1935 to 11 November 1936

LOCATION OF BUILDING
Meridian and Ohio Streets

for any federal building, new or old. Thus, the downtown post office and courthouse in Indianapolis qualified for decoration. Because of the competition sketches he had submitted, Grant Christian was hired to prepare designs for an area outside the third-floor courtroom and to hire one or more assistants to help him paint the seven panels. Also as opposed to the Section's program, employment by TRAP gave the individual a weekly salary, based on a thirty-hour week, four weeks a month. For the master artist this amounted to $1.55 per hour, while the assistants earned 77.5 cents per hour. This was not "make work" or "boondoggle" employment, however; it was legitimate decoration of a federal building, but an older building that did not qualify for decoration under the other programs.

When the first issue of the Section's monthly *Bulletin* was issued on 1 March 1935 C. J. Peoples, director of the Procurement Division, discussed the goals of the program:

> Without being sentimental, the Section of Painting and Sculpture hopes that in employing the vital talents of this country, faith in the country and a renewed sense of its glorious possibilities will be awakened both in the artists and in their audiences, and that through this the Section will do its full share in the development of the art and the spiritual life of the United States of America.

In an interview in 1978 Christian echoed that same feeling when asked about the importance of the art projects to him and to other artists of the time:

> I think it was an extremely important thing. It created a lot of interest in our heritage. I think people were a little closer together because of it. There were more farm folk; there was a lot of upheaval and turmoil. It was quite a period of transition with all the hardships that people went through in losing farms and trying just to feed [themselves].

Grant Christian also painted *Waiting for the Mail* for Nappanee in 1938.

Although not every commission for a post office mural came as the result of a winning entry in a competition, the overwhelming majority did come either because the artist won the competition or was awarded an honorable mention, which usually led to an invitation to submit sketches for another, probably smaller, post office in a different location.

In 1938 a regional competition was held for artists "resident of or attached to the states of Michigan and Indiana" for commissions to be awarded for the East Detroit post office and the Jasper post office. In that contest Jessie Hull Mayer won the commission for Jasper, while Frank Cassara was given the award for East Detroit. Two other Indiana artists received invitations to submit sketches for possible commissions as a result of this two-state competition: Jean Swiggett of Franklin for the Franklin post office and William Kaeser of Indianapolis for the Pendleton post office.

Even during what proved to be the busiest years for the Section, 1938 and 1939, the Section tried to hold as many competitions as possible. Section *Bulletin* No. 18 for February 1939 announced a national mural competition for St. Louis; a regional sculpture competition for Los Angeles, open to sculptors in states west of the Mississippi

TITLE
Indiana Farming Scene in Late Autumn

SIZE
11'4" x 4'

ARTIST
Jessie Hull Mayer

FEE
$650

BASIS FOR THE AWARD
Won a regional competition for post offices in Jasper, Indiana, and in East Detroit, Michigan

MEDIUM
Oil on canvas

DATES
Contract 4 January 1939 for 230 calendar days
Postmaster letter confirming installation, 8 August 1939

LOCATION OF BUILDING
206 East Sixth Street

River; a mural competition for Amarillo, Texas, open to artists from Arkansas, Colorado, Kansas, Louisiana, Mississippi, Missouri, New Mexico, Oklahoma, and Texas; a mural competition for Wilmington, North Carolina, open to artists from the District of Columbia, Maryland, North Carolina, South Carolina, and Virginia; a local mural competition for the Poughkeepsie, New York, post office, open only to artists in Ulster and Duchess Counties, New York; and a "competition limited to Kentucky artists for the Berea Post Office."

A Treasury Department press release cited the elements in Mayer's proposed mural design that attracted the committee's attention:

> Mrs. Mayer's winning design depicts an autumn day on an Indiana farm. The design in the opinion of the local jury, "Has a charming decorative pattern and reflects a keen personal observation of the elements of her subject matter." On the left of the design the farmers are loading a crop of pumpkins into a wagon. Black and white cows are arranged in interesting pattern on a near hill. The farmer's wife opens a letter at the mail box and her young son rushes from the house to hear the news. The house, barns and trees are typical of the region.

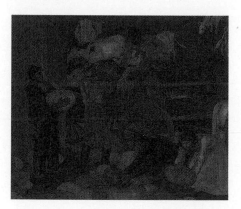

The Jasper design has one unusual feature, two small "cartouches," three feet wide by one foot high panels under the main portion of the mural, bordering the postmaster's door, with drawings of airmail bags, guns, and corn shocks. Also to Mayer's credit is that although her file in the National Archives in Washington is full, little of the paperwork relates to the Jasper mural, based upon the fact that it had been through the public competition process and upon her basic competency as an artist.

In its efforts to make art and artists as real and as much a part of the community as possible, the Section often provided biographical information about winning artists.

> Jessie Hull Mayer who won the competition for the decoration of the Jasper, Indiana Post Office was born in New Haven, Connecticut,

July 1910. She received the degree, Bachelor of Fine Arts at Yale School of Fine Arts in 1932. The same year she was married to Henrik Martin Mayer. She and her husband lived in New York for a year and since then have made their home in Indianapolis, Indiana where she has painted mostly water colors. One-man shows of her work including water colors, oils and mural designs have been shown in Indiana and Louisville, Kentucky.

The Jasper commission was Mayer's second Indiana work, preceded by *The Arrival of the Mail in Culver* in 1938 and followed by *The Corn School* for Lagrange in 1941.

"The church, the saloon and the stage coach were vital things in the early history of Knightstown." Thus did Raymond L. Morris end his descriptive narrative about his mural for the post office in Knightstown, the only town named for Jonathan Knight, the federal surveyor who laid out the National Road through Knightstown and the rest of Indiana. The highway brought settlers in covered wagons and travelers and the mail in stagecoaches.

According to the histories, and the stories told to me, Knightstown was settled by the Quakers, and was soon invaded by another element, which caused trouble there for many years. It is located on the old National Road and the arrival of the stage coach was the biggest event of the day.

In a sense Morris's commission for a mural on the National Road, so closely identified with the development of Indiana as a state, is apt for a man who did not decide to become a painter until he was thirty-six years old and who attended the Chicago World's Fair in 1933, where he was captivated by the Thomas Hart Benton murals in the Indiana pavilion:

TITLE
The Evening Mail

SIZE
12' x 5'

ARTIST
Raymond L. Morris

FEE
$560

BASIS FOR THE AWARD
"Designs submitted in competition"

MEDIUM
Oil on canvas

DATES
Contract 14 October 1937 for 229 calendar days
Postmaster letter confirming installation, 3 March 1938

LOCATION OF BUILDING
37 North Jefferson Street

When I came home I had definitely made up my mind to do the thing I had always wanted to do. The following January I started in [John Herron Art] school and I have worked continually, seven days a week, since that time. I never tire of it, get a kick out of it, and believe I know definitely what I want to do.

Prior to that time he had studied engineering for one year before serving in the navy in World War I, took a "Dry Kiln Engineering correspondence course" from the University of Wisconsin and a business administration degree from LaSalle University in Chicago. He studied under Henrik Martin Mayer and Donald Mattison at Herron for three and one-half years, while occasionally taking "a night drawing class at Elmer Taflinger's." The culmination of all his effort was the invitation letter from Edward B. Rowan on 22 July 1937 to submit sketches for the Knightstown mural.

Originally the artist wanted to do the mural "in tempera direct on the wall. Of course I would mount sheeting on the wall and gesso it to paint on." At the time the contract was written, however, Morris had switched to a more standard oil on canvas approach. By the time the mural was mounted on the wall Morris had made at least a dozen major changes to satisfy the Section staff once the 8″ x 10″ photograph of the full-size cartoon was received in Washington. Rowan's 10 January 1938 letter carried instructions:

> Kindly check the scale and length of the raised arm of the woman on the left; check the drawing of lower extremities of the near man seated on the coach. . . . The hindquarters of the central horse should also be studied further, supplemented by observation from nature. . . . It is suggested that the church be moved slightly left in the composition. The line of the foot of the running boy with the base line of the portmanteau carried by the traveler should be broken.

Observation of the photograph of the cartoon and of the finished mural will show that Morris faithfully carried out every one of these suggestions, regardless of how minor they may seem.

One behavior depicted in the design, that of the two men fighting in the right center background, seems somehow out of place. All the other activity is related to the arrival of the stage, whether it is the man slowing down the horses, the persons waving at the arrivals, or the couple standing at the extreme right who probably will board the stage when it leaves. But why are the two men fighting, and why is everyone else ignoring them? The answer comes in another part of Rowan's January letter:

> It is also suggested that the title "Jack's Saloon" be omitted or some other title be substituted such as "Jack's Place." The word Saloon appearing so prominently is apt to bring comments on the part of citizens of Knightstown and frankly we do not feel that the word saloon should be so prominent. Anyone looking at the building will recognize the establishment without benefit of the label.

And, dutifully, when the artist painted the final canvas the very prominent "Jack's Saloon" is missing from the wall of the building in the background.

When Morris wrote to Rowan on 20 February 1938 to tell him the mural had been installed, the artist was quite proud of his work. "Everyone who has seen this likes the man stopping the horses and the boy in front of them and the horses." The postmaster's letter on 3 March underscored that appreciation:

> I think Mr. Morris is to be congratulated on this work and it has received much favorable local attention and comment.
>
> The scene is characteristic of Knightstown as it might have well appeared one hundred years ago on the arrival of the stage coach, which was at that time our only contact with the outside and for this reason is particularly appropriate to be hung in the post office.

Later in March Morris wrote to Rowan asking if he thought it would be worth it to move to Texas for the upcoming Dallas post office competition, a national competition. Never one to mince words, Rowan replied on 2 April 1938.

> I do not advise such action on two counts: first, there will be future mural competitions in which you will be eligible without going to this undue expense and secondly, the competition with other able artists will, in my estimation, be too keen for you to hope to win. The latter statement is based upon my study of the photographs of your work.

Raymond L. Morris did not receive any other commissions from the Section of Fine Arts.

For Indiana, it all began in Lafayette; here was the first competition in Indiana, the first mural commission in Indiana, and the first mural installed in Indiana.

On 5 January 1935 Edward B. Rowan, superintendent, Section of Painting and Sculpture, Procurement Division, Department of the Treasury, sent a letter to Walter Scholer, architect of the new post office in Lafayette, inviting him to become a member of a committee charged with the responsibility of conducting a competition to select an artist to paint murals for this building. Previously O. L. Foster, president of the Lafayette Art Association, was invited to chair the committee but declined, and the position then was offered to Wilbur D. Peat, director of the John Herron Art Institute in Indianapolis. Peat accepted the invitation "with considerable reluctance," but admitted that "in view of my interest in the Public Works of Art Project, I do not see how I can gracefully decline."

In the four and one-half pages of his letter to Peat, Rowan spelled out the details of the contest. Since the amount of funding available was less than five thousand dollars, Rowan said the competition would be a local one "in the region where the work is to be finally installed." Had the funding been for more than five thousand dollars, the competition would have been held on a national basis.

> The exact geographical limitations of the regions to be covered by this competition we will leave largely to your good judgment. The regions should be sufficiently large to include all of the artists who would naturally look to Lafayette, Indiana as an art center, and in a general way we would suggest that no artists who submit designs be turned down because of their place of residence. State lines can be ignored.

Later competitions would have much stricter guidelines, but in 1935 the Section was just beginning and did not realize all the restraints and strictures it would have to apply to have control of the process in later years.

One of the most delightful anecdotes to come from this competition was the revelation, for Washington, D.C., that two qualified artists with the same last name could reside at the same address: Henrik Martin Mayer, who won the competition with his mail delivery designs, and Jessie Hull Mayer, who was official runner-up with other "postal activity" designs. Rowan wrote to Peat after all the designs had been sent to Washington, especially complimenting Jessie Hull Mayer's sketches:

> I wonder if she by any chance is the wife of Mr. Henrik Martin Mayer. It hardly seems likely that two such competent artists would be members of the same family.

TITLE
Rural Delivery and *Sad News*

SIZE
2 at 3' x 7'6"

ARTIST
Henrik Martin Mayer

FEE
$700

BASIS FOR THE AWARD
Won Lafayette competition

MEDIUM
Oil on canvas

DATES
Contract 28 September 1935 for 276 calendar days

Chair of competition letter confirming installation, 13 July 1936

LOCATION OF BUILDING
230 North Fourth Street

Eventually Rowan asked Jessie Hull Mayer the same questions, and as reported elsewhere, she replied, apparently facetiously, that "it perhaps is best for the peace of our family that you did not award it to me, because I am Mrs. Henrik Martin Mayer." At one point the two of them came close to receiving a joint appointment for the Lafayette lobby, when Rowan tried to hire Jessie Hull Mayer under the TRAP program. "Would you mind telling me if by any chance you are eligible for relief employment; if so, it might be quite possible for us to consider carrying out revised designs of your sketches under a relief employment program." Apparently Rowan wanted to hire her to put her designs up in the lobby along with her husband's, probably qualifying him as master artist and her as assistant. Since Henrik Martin Mayer was assistant director of the John Herron Art Institute, the Mayers did not qualify for relief, and the plan got nowhere.

Another interesting aspect of the "Mayer and Mayer" anecdote pertains to Rowan's disbelief that more than one qualified person could have the same last name or the same address, unless one person had acquired the name by marriage. In 1938 Jenne and Ethel Magafan, twins living in Colorado, were runners-up in two different competitions, and between 1938 and 1942 "the Magafan sisters," as they came to be known in the Section, received a total of seven mural commissions.

When Rowan sent the original letters to Peat and to Scholer asking them to be members of the selection committee, he made it clear that although they would conduct the competition and would look at the entries and choose the top drawings, their opinions were strictly advisory to the Section, and ultimately, to the supervising architect in the Treasury's Procurement Division. Thus, when, in fact, "Mr. Stone, the Acting Supervising Architect," questioned a shadow as cast by the eaves of the barn in one of Mayer's designs, that criticism dutifully went on to the artist, who answered on 5 July 1936:

The only comment I can make on the criticism of the cast shadow under the eaves on the right side of the barn is to agree with you. According to the true laws of cast shadows it would not show. I took artist's liberties, if there is such a thing, in distorting a bit in order to strengthen that particular line in the composition. I could remove it but I feel that then the line of the eaves would be too thin to carry from the floor. Sometimes, I believe liberties of this kind can be taken. Veronese, as you no doubt know, sometimes used several points of perspective in one picture to serve his purpose. It seems to me that some things which look distorted at a small scale naturally adjust themselves at the full scale. Since I received your letter I have tried to get the reactions of a number of persons on this point and find that at full scale this shadow does not trouble

anyone. I will remove it if you think best; my only reason for wanting to keep it as it is, is to keep the strength of that line of the eaves
great enough to repeat that made by the ornate eaves of the house
in the other panel.

Rowan sent a letter back to Mayer:

The criticism relative to the cast shadows under the eaves on the
right side of the barn was, as you probably guessed, not my personal
criticism, but was offered by one of the members of the Division,
and it is our policy to submit such criticisms to the artists for
their consideration.

   The explanation which you give in your letter is one with which
I wholeheartedly agree, and the members of the Section are ready
to support you in this if in the full scale cartoon you feel it essential
to your design to take this minor liberty with the laws of nature.

   I have every confidence in you as a creative artist, and want
you to feel free to work out your problem in accordance with your
own wishes.

No other negative critical comments were offered to Mayer about
his bending of "the laws of nature." In fact, when Wilbur Peat wrote
Rowan after the murals were installed, his letter contained nothing
but praise:

There is another factor about Mayer's work that I feel is important
in this connection: he hits a nice balance between the careful, "realistic" rendering of the objects, and a personal interpretation of his
material; so that the work can be grasped by the public generally,
and still receive the admiration of people looking for the artistic
elements in the work.

Henrik Martin Mayer also prepared *Down to the Ferry* for Aurora
in 1938.

TITLE
The Corn School

SIZE
11'2" x 5'7"

ARTIST
Jessie Hull Mayer

FEE
$750

BASIS FOR THE AWARD
"Competent design submitted in 48-State Competition"

MEDIUM
Oil on canvas

DATES
Contract 2 June 1941 for 191 calendar days

Postmaster letter confirming installation, 24 November 1941

LOCATION OF BUILDING
300 South Detroit Street

S hortly before the mural was installed Edward B. Rowan wrote to Jessie Hull Mayer in praise of the work, saying "the whole thing is quite alive and I regard this painting as your finest work that I have yet seen." Without doubt, the Lagrange mural is a complex and sophisticated work of art, which, according to the postmaster brought "a quick smile of recognition . . . to the faces of patrons as they come into the lobby and they then linger to study further interesting details."

On 21 April 1941 Mayer included a description of Lagrange and the mural when she sent the two-inch color sketch required before her contract could be written.

Lagrange is the county seat of a completely agricultural locality. The land is extremely fertile and well cared for, especially by the numerous Amish, who are skillful and thrifty farmers. The Postmaster warned me against using Amish subject matter as "they are not considered assets to the community," alas. However I am going to put a few in the crowd of people in my mural.

The subject matter I have taken is that of the livestock parade at the county fair, held in Lagrange and called "Corn School." It is quite an affair, lasting a week, held on the courthouse square which is closed to traffic and filled with display tents and amusement concessions. This is characteristic of most county fairs in Indiana. I have shown the courthouse as background, of red brick and white wood, so much handsomer and more appropriate to its locality than the usual newer county courthouses, heavily marbled and ponderously Renaissance. The animals I have shown are characteristic. Percheron and Belgian horses, Hereford cattle shown by 4-H club members, fine wool sheep, dusted with ochre. Somehow I couldn't show all this to you at a small scale in the black and white of a pencil sketch. This is why I have sent no preliminary small drawings. I had made so many, I became confused, and dove right into color. . . .

The walls are creams, the wainscot and woodwork warm gray, colours which would harmonize with any mural colour scheme.

I hope you will like the design. I eagerly await the opinion and comments of the Section of Fine Arts.

Eighteen of the Indiana murals are found in county seat locations, each, obviously, with a county courthouse. During the nineteenth century every county in Indiana built at least one new courthouse, many of them expressive of classical or mansard-roofed models. Only three of the Indiana post office muralists chose to feature the courthouse in their designs: Henrik Martin Mayer in Lafayette, Tom Rost in Paoli, and Jessie Hull Mayer in Lagrange. However, only Jessie Hull Mayer makes the building a focal point in the center background, all "red brick and white wood, so much handsomer and more appropriate to its locality than the usual newer county courthouses, heavily marbled and ponderously Renaissance."

The "Corn School," which gave its name both to the painting and to the fair, commemorates the time about 1907 when faculty from Purdue University would visit Lagrange each fall to help the farmers choose corn for seeds the following year. Until the science of agronomy reached the point where hybrid seeds could be produced year after year with all the desirable traits of several different plants combined into one, the choosing of planting stock for each spring was a form of guesswork and experience. Thus the professors would get together each year with the farmers after the crops were in to choose those ears of corn that looked most healthy, most resistant to blight of one kind or another, for use as seed for the next spring. In 1911 the farmers began to bring in other examples of farm produce and added a parade. About 1913 the carnival became a function of the event as it developed into a typical county fair. Even after the farmers no longer needed the help of the academicians each year, the "Corn School" lent its name and part of the reason for its existence to the county fair shown in Jessie Hull Mayer's mural.

The Lagrange mural also has the dubious distinction of being one of the two murals in Indiana which were inappropriately "repaired" after damage. In the right-hand foreground a woman sits with a child in her lap, just before or inside the small display tent. Her facial characteristics are not like the other persons in the mural, and her bright pink dress clashes with the muted tones of the panel. This "correction," done by a local painter, and one or two other smaller repairs came as a result of water damage to the mural.

When the mural was installed the postmaster wrote to Washington to confirm the acceptability of the painting:

> So far as I know the picture was placed properly. The painting itself is very pleasing, and, I believe, surpasses the expectations of the general public.
>
> With the county court house as a background, a quick smile of recognition comes to the faces of patrons as they come into the lobby and then they linger to study further interesting details. With few exceptions all comments heard are very, very good.
>
> This building has a very beautiful lobby and it is further enhanced by the fine mural. Mrs. Mayer, in my opinion, did a good piece of work.

Jessie Hull Mayer's three Indiana post office lobby murals show an interesting development both in terms of technical ability and in terms of a regionalist, American Scene narrative. Her first work, *The Arrival of the Mail in Culver*, has a central panel depicting many different community units receiving the mail, but still has six separate side panels showing other aspects of the community, ranging from recreational activities on Lake Maxinkuckee to the Culver Military Academy. Her second work, *Indiana Farming Scene in Late Autumn*, in Jasper, is a well-developed, lyrical farmscape with no indication of the town. In Lagrange she brings together all the disparate members of the community into one panel, bringing farmers and farm animals to the streets of the town where the residents can view the "Corn School" and its parade.

Her fourth Section mural is *Winter Landscape*, painted for Canton, Missouri, in 1940.

TITLE
Autumn Fields

SIZE
12'3" x 4'3"

ARTIST
Avery Johnson

FEE
$670

BASIS OF THE AWARD
*"Designs submitted in Interior
Department Competition"*

MEDIUM
Oil on canvas

DATES
*Contract 15 December 1938 for
259 calendar days*
*Postmaster letter confirming
installation, 21 July 1939*

LOCATION OF BUILDING
29 East Union Street

I f there is a "sleeper" in the Indiana post office mural collection, *Autumn Fields* in Liberty probably is it. This mural of no specific place and no specific time, other than "autumn," is a quintessential Midwest mural.

During the 1930s much was written about Regionalism and about "regionalism," that is, the style of art popularized and promoted by Thomas Hart Benton, John Steuart Curry, and Grant Wood—Regionalism—and the sociological/political/geographical idea of location—the Midwest, New England, the South, etc. The Section promoted the latter through its insistence that artists visit the locale of their commissions to seek appropriate local content for sketches while at the same time promoting the former art style by insisting upon "American Scene" content in funded murals.

A survey of the murals produced for the Section in the various parts of the country will show a commonality based upon geographic location. In the East, whether New England or Middle Atlantic states, the majority of murals evince a local history conception as the guiding principle, but the local twist usually meant that history was closely tied to the early history of the nation. That is, many murals depict Revolutionary War battles or skirmishes with British tax collectors in colonial days or the arrival of the first immigrants to the New World.

In the South history was a problem because so much of the past associated with the South involved slavery and the Civil War, neither of which was an allowable topic for mural commissions. Many of the southern murals then have an agricultural content, with the focus usually on cotton or tobacco. In the West the emphasis often is upon Native Americans, with or without the involvement of white settlers, or the Spanish heritage of the regions, or the modern cowboy.

In the Midwest the murals also reflect a local history, but it is a history of agricultural or industrial development, the growth of the community, or the arrival of immigrants who will provide the labor, whether on the farm or in the factory. The Midwest murals really do portray an agricultural and industrial "heartland" of the nation, whether given a specific geographic location, as in *Building the Industrial Foundation of Batesville* or *From Such Beginnings Sprang the County of Lake, Indiana,* in Crown Point or, as Johnson said of his mural:

> The subject of this mural is a familiar sight to anyone who has travelled through the farmlands of the middle west, where it is repeated countless times in slightly varying form. It is so familiar in fact, that it becomes easy to overlook its significance, for no historic event ever happened here, no battles fought, no treaties signed. It is simply a Southern Indiana Farm, yet one of the most vital segments of our national life; a one family farm truly representing the American ideals of individual independence and democratic cooperation.
>
> In southern Indiana, lying as it does between the hills and mountains to eastward and the flat plains farther west, is found a gently rolling terrain whose contours are particularly fluent and rhythmic in their undulations. It is this quality which has been used as the design basis for the mural.

When Avery Johnson began work on this mural, the second of six which he did for the Section, Edward B. Rowan thought a rural scene would be appropriate, and Johnson immediately responded: "I'm glad you suggested rural subject matter, as a good mid-west farm scene is just the sort of thing I'd like to do on this job." He submitted four pencil sketches to the Section for comment, all of which were liked by the staff:

> The two which were regarded as most unusual were those entitled Autumn Fields and Loading Hay. . . . It is our suggestion that you develop your preference of these two into a two-inch scale color sketch.

That kind of latitude—"you develop your preference"—was very unusual and reflected both the belief the Section had in Johnson's ability and the quality of the sketches.

As a visit to Liberty will show today, Johnson chose "Autumn Fields," and the local clientele responded favorably. Even the newspapers were complimentary in their coverage:

> The artist's interpretation of local agricultural land is portrayed, although he stated that no specific field or building is included in the scene. Painted in colors harmonizing with the decorative scheme of the post office, the picture shows rolling farm land, a roadway between two farms, and fields filled with ripened grain.
>
> Mr. Johnson received inspiration for the picture while traveling through the southern part of Indiana last autumn.

Avery Johnson also painted *Industrial Marseilles* for Marseilles, Illinois, in 1938; *Skating on Bonaparte's Pond* for Bordentown, New Jersey, in 1940; *Chicot County Wild Life* for Lake Village, Arkansas, in 1941; *Purchase of Territory of North Bergen from the Indians* for North Bergen, New Jersey, in 1942; and *Incidents in the History of Catonsville* for Catonsville, Maryland, in 1942.

LIGONIER IN
MAR 15
19

TITLE
Cutting Timber

SIZE
13'11" x 5'3"

ARTIST
Fay E. Davis

FEE
$1,000

BASIS FOR THE AWARD
"Designs submitted in St. Louis Competition"

MEDIUM
Oil on canvas

DATES
Contract 15 March 1940 for 260 calendar days

Postmaster letter confirming installation, 10 September 1940

LOCATION OF BUILDING
201 South Main Street

For Fay E. Davis the Section of Fine Arts provided an auspicious beginning for her career. After five years at the John Herron Art Institute, all on full scholarship, she received her Bachelor of Fine Arts degree in June 1939. By November of that year she had received two invitations to submit sketches for murals, one in Ligonier and one in Chester, Illinois.

After a visit to Ligonier, Davis submitted at least two ideas to Washington for the mural, one a farm scene and one the timber scene. Edward B. Rowan chose the latter in his 19 March 1940 letter:

> [W]e were particularly impressed with the design of the lumber scene. The oxen pulling the carts with logs on the right seemed particularly well conceived and I want to congratulate you on the sense of place which you have achieved in this section of the design. The activities indicated on the left are also satisfactory but it is suggested that the functional actions of the men, in sawing through the tree, should be authenticated. It may be necessary for you to relegate the burning of the brush further into the background in this section.

A few weeks later Davis eased the accuracy concerns of the Washington staff:

> I took [the sketch] to one of my acquaintances who is a lumber-jack. He gave me some information on the cutting of timber and told me in what way to make the design authentic.

The scene that she portrays presents a mixed message, at first one of profligacy and waste, but one also of progress and conservation. The left and center background of the painting is filled with the scene of wood being burned, that is, being wasted. Yet the right background shows logs cut and loaded on a cart, obviously to be shipped elsewhere.

The settlers around Ligonier were presented with a dichotomy: they needed to clear the land for farming but had no market for most of the woodlands they cleared. That is, much of the woods were composed of noncommercially useful timber that was either too soft or too stunted for building purposes. The timber and brush simply had to be removed so that planting could begin. The best way to remove it was by burning, and that is what the artist shows in the left and center background. On the other hand, older growth timber that had commercial value was harvested and, according to the artist, "shipped to the east for ship building."

The oxen are quite well executed, especially the darker one in the rear; an anthropomorphic reading of the painting would say that this particular ox is happy in its work for it almost seems to be smiling. In addition, the swirling flames and the flowing lines of the oxen and the human figures give a great vitality to the painting.

In 1941 Davis moved to Chicago to pursue her career, feeling that the big city would provide more "opportunity for mental growth, progress and inspiration," which would warrant "the extra expense" of city living. Because of that expense she wrote to Rowan asking for information about a possible competition for Columbus, Indiana, which never took place, and about possible employment on WPA art projects of one kind or another. "Thus far with two mural commissions I have done very well. But the money earned will soon be gone."

She did receive, later that year, another commission, this one for Oglesby, Illinois, *The Illini and Pottowatomies Struggling at Starved Rock*. This Illinois work depicts the battle between these two tribes, which gave "starved rock" its name. Ironically, this mural was to cause a minor ruckus in 1993 when one of the postal employees who cleaned the lobby objected to the nude buttocks of the Native Americans depicted in the mural, saying they were offensive to him, becoming a kind of "sexual harassment." For a while the mural was covered with two venetian blinds that would be raised for anyone who asked to see the mural but had to be lowered after the viewing. Eventually a judge ruled that the scantily clothed American Indian figures did not constitute harassment, and the blinds were removed.

As mentioned above, Fay E. Davis prepared three murals for the Section: Ligonier in 1940; *Loading the Packet*, a river scene, for Chester, Illinois, also in 1940; and the 1942 Oglesby Indian scene.

TITLE
The Arrival of the Mail

SIZE
16' x 5'6"

ARTIST
Alan Tompkins

FEE
$610

BASIS FOR THE AWARD
*Sketches submitted for the Justice
Department competition*

MEDIUM
Oil on canvas

DATES
*Contract 1 December 1936 for
365 calendar days*

*Postmaster letter confirming
installation, 26 July 1937*

LOCATION OF BUILDING
10 South Main Street

The Martinsville mural presents a concern to be faced by all those who wish to preserve these artworks. If any damage occurs to the mural, the repairs must be sensitively done and done only in the spirit of the original work. That is, the mural should be "restored" to match as closely as possible its appearance at the time of installation. It should not be "redone" to meet the desires of a later painter. Indiana has two examples where the person brought in to repair damage did not do so in a manner true to the commissioned artist's desire, Martinsville and Lagrange.

When Tompkins was invited to submit sketches for the Martinsville mural, he was pleased and excited to be chosen, as he recalled in a 1978 interview:

As one of the artists who benefited [from the federal programs] I know that since I was just out of Yale at the time I got the first commission [for Martinsville], I wouldn't have had similar commissions at that time if it hadn't been for the program. It made available suddenly these relatively small commissions in very good buildings, but not major buildings, and it taught the artists their relationship to society and made them think about society's needs in a way that I don't know any other program has done since.

For Tompkins the mural was an unequaled opportunity to do something appropriate for the community. His ideas, he said, came "from visiting the locales like Martinsville and trying to get a feel of the town, what the people were like, what kind of people they were, farmers or tradesmen or whatever." His goal from all the research was to do a mural "which seemed to me at that time to suit the surroundings, to suit the post office there."

That desire to create a work appropriate for Martinsville in 1937 became the key to his entire effort. From the beginning he had decided upon a "somber" palette for the work, which the Section staff misinterpreted as a desire by the artist to key "the tone of the mural too closely to the plaster painting and the woodwork of the lobby." On the contrary, his inclination was based upon his training at the Yale Art School, where he was taught "that a mural should not grab the attention like a billboard, that it ought to meld into its surroundings, and reward attention only when attention was given it, but never shout for attention." A letter from Edward B. Rowan, dated 21 April 1937, again called attention to the color scheme:

> We still feel you could enliven the general tone of this rather than keeping the entire decoration so somber. Your work shows that you are an experienced colorist, but I do not feel that you have treated your theme in a lively palette. Your scheme reflects the mood of the woman going down the steps much more decidedly than it does that of the central group reading the letter of good news.

In the 1978 interview Tompkins said, "I think I can say those were pretty somber-color days for me, and it [the mural] was in umbers and darker tones."

The artist's original, undated letter to the Section explains what he desired to achieve and why:

> The scene represents a porch of a Post Office in the typical small American town. The central figure has received a letter of good news and his family and friends join in the surge of good feeling and well wishing which accompanies such an event. The figure of secondary interest, the woman descending the steps at the right, symbolizes the receiver of tragic news. Alone and speechless in her grief, she is not approached by others in the community. Nevertheless the group of townspeople at the extreme right exhibit a concern

and sympathy for her. The two figures at the extreme left of the composition in the half light of anticipation have not learned the nature of the news contained in their letter, and serve therefore as an introduction to the extremes of joy and grief in the other groups.

> In general I have tried to convey a sense of the warmth and genuineness of friendly interest in others in American community life as well as an idea of the importance of the mails in the daily drama of our existence.

In 1974 a fire in the post office caused smoke damage to the mural, and a local painter, A. Raemaekers, was hired to restore the work. As Raemaekers told the author in a 1976 interview, "I always felt the colors were too dark," so when given the chance he repainted the mural in brighter colors, including intense reds and blues.

When Tompkins was told about the changed color scheme in Martinsville, he reiterated his original desire to convey a somewhat melancholy impression in the work:

> I think one of the reasons was the feeling of the earthiness of the town, of its farming, even of the people—the opposite of what I had been used to, the sort of dressed-up atmosphere of New York City— I think it impressed me that these people were close to the soil, and the types in the mural would lead you to understand that. And I don't think bright colors would go with it at all. I imagine it's pretty well wrecked. . . . I wanted something that would stay in its place and not intrude, so that many people would use the post office room without ever noticing it and go about their business untroubled by it. But if they took occasion to look at it and study it, they would be rewarded by the detail and the interest.

Today, more than two decades after the 1974 repainting, dirt and aging have reduced some of the inappropriate brightness, and the mural begins again to resemble its 1937 incarnation, but this misdirected effort at changing anything about the artist's original work and the artist's response to that change should serve as a warning to others who are similarly tempted.

Tompkins installed this mural in 1937; *Indiana Farm—Sunday Afternoon* for North Manchester in 1938; and *Suburban Street* in the Broad Ripple station in Indianapolis in 1942.

TITLE
Early Middlebury Mail

SIZE
12' x 5'1"

ARTIST
Raymond Redell

FEE
$670

BASIS FOR THE AWARD
"Competent work performed for the Section of Painting and Sculpture"

MEDIUM
Oil on canvas

DATES
Contract 4 January 1939 for 208 calendar days

Postmaster letter confirming installation, 26 June 1939

LOCATION OF BUILDING
200 South Main Street

Of the thirty-seven murals installed in Indiana post office lobbies, about a dozen have delivery of the mail as either their central theme or as one of the major elements of the design. In midwestern states about one-third of all the murals depict postal activities. So many post office-related themes led some artists to accuse their colleagues of "painting Section," that is, of submitting designs which may have been second-rate and/or deliberately schmaltzy just to increase their chances of winning the competition. Perhaps some artists did, in fact, try to "hedge their bets," as it were, by catering to local juries, which always included the postmaster and a local historian or librarian or to national authorities, since the Fourth Assistant Postmaster General had to approve the installation of every mural. At the same time at least one or two postmasters did, in fact, prohibit the cementing of the finished murals to lobby walls because of their supposedly inappropriate or inaccurate content. With all that to consider, and with the fact that the federal government, which included the Post Office Department, was paying the bill, why shouldn't an artist try to conceive of an idea that immediately would be complimentary and pleasing to the patron? At the same time, shouldn't an artist look to please the viewing public as well by providing a painting that aggrandizes the local history or businesses and industries, if such can be done without blatant glorification?

None of the artists who painted the Indiana murals has ever spoken of feeling any pressure to "paint Section," so the contemporary viewer who wonders about the large number of postmen and mail carriers shown can simply chalk it up to appropriate designs for the location. In fact, when Redell visited Middlebury he was given a copy of the 1936 centennial edition of the local newspaper as a working document for mural design sketches. Certainly he would have been remiss had he refused to consider those ideas for his mural and, in fact, as he told the Section, his final design idea came from a story in the paper about the first mail delivery, and that later became the basis for the Section's press release:

> The subject matter for this mural was inspired by an excerpt from the Centennial Edition of the "Middlebury Independent" newspaper. According to this account, John Bockus drove the first mail wagon from Middlebury to Vistula. Beside the driver sat a rider armed with a heavy rifle to ward off attacks. Passengers inside the coach were a lady and children.

Redell's file also reveals one aspect of the whole program most viewers do not think about: how was the mural attached to the wall? On 5 May 1939 the artist wrote to the postmaster:

> I intend to install the mural for your postoffice on June 11, which is on a Sunday. This is the only convenient day of the week for me; could you arrange to give me access to the lobby all day?
>
> During my visit to your postoffice you mentioned you would arrange with a painter to do work for me. In order to save a special trip down could you give him these instructions: Remove the paint from the wall over your door to the moulding under the ceiling and down to the bulletin boards. . . . This should be done 3 weeks before installation of the mural, about the 18th or 19th of May. (This is important in order to give the wall a chance to dry thoroughly. I believe casein paint is removed by soaking with warm water. I think the painter will know how to remove it.) If he has any trouble removing the paint I would like to be notified immediately.
>
> Then 2 weeks later he should apply one coat of this sizing: 1 part alcohol, 1 part shellac. (This will have 1 week to dry thoroughly.)

> If you can find a painter who can give me about 2 or 3 hours of his time and help and the use of his scaffolding and ladders on June 11 will you send me his rough estimate for the total amount of work?

He added a P.S. to explain further:

> The canvas that the painting is on is to be pasted on the wall . . . and cannot be put on over casein paint. This is why the paint has to be removed.

On 10 May the postmaster replied:

> I . . . have got in touch with the painter that did the work here and he informs me that the lobby has an oil base paint (2 coats) and not a casein coat as was suggested when you were here. . . .
>
> Mr. Blough (the painter) was under the impression you would not want this removed; however if you will let me know just how you wish the oil paint taken care of the painter will do same.
>
> Mr. Blough will be glad to help you on June 11 and will have his scaffolding and ladders on hand. I asked him as to his charges and he stated about 75 cents an hour. You will find him very reasonable. Anything you wish looking after just feel free to ask.

That solved all the problems, and on 11 June 1939 Redell, a friend, and Mr. Blough installed *Early Middlebury Mail* on the wall of the lobby. On 26 June the postmaster, Ben E. Wise, wrote to the Procurement Division of the Treasury:

> Am more than pleased to report that Mr. Raymond Redell installed the mural at this office on June 11, 1939.
>
> Personally I think that this mural is an exceptionally fine piece of workmanship and from the numerous comments I hear I think that the public is of the same opinion. . . .
>
> On behalf of the P. O. employees, this community, and myself I want to thank the Procurement Division for this fine work of Art, as it certainly adds a very definite touch to our new P. O. Building, of which the whole community is very proud.

Raymond Redell also produced *Gathering Cranberries* for Berlin, Wisconsin, in 1938 and *Wisconsin Countryside* for Waupaca, Wisconsin, in 1940.

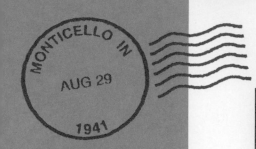

TITLE
Hay Making

SIZE
14′6″ x 8′6″

ARTIST
Marguerite Zorach

FEE
$800

BASIS FOR THE AWARD
*Designs submitted in War
Department Building competition*

MEDIUM
Oil on canvas

DATES
*Contract 29 August 1941 for
336 calendar days*

*Postmaster letter confirming
installation, 14 November 1942*

LOCATION OF BUILDING
125 West Broadway Street

Marguerite Zorach received the official contract for the Monticello post office mural a few days before her fifty-fourth birthday, making her one of the older artists who received commissions during the Section's eight-year existence. As such she represented an earlier style of artist training than that of many of the younger artists just starting out in the 1930s.

For example, rather than spending only six months or a year in Europe after graduating from art school, a trip usually funded by a scholarship or prize of some sort, as was the case with most of the younger Indiana mural artists, Zorach spent four years in Europe, 1908-1912. She returned before the post–World War I "expatriate" artists and writers had even thought much about going abroad.

Zorach exhibited in the famous (or infamous, depending upon one's view) Armory Show of 1913. That show had a section devoted to avant-garde European painters and was the introduction for most Americans to the works of artists such as Pablo Picasso and Marcel Duchamp, whose *Nude Descending a Staircase, No. 2* brought howls of derision from professionals and amateurs alike, with Theodore Roosevelt calling it *Explosion in a Shingle Factory,* for example. She also disliked what she called the "Dean Cornwell School" of commercial art, feeling such artists should not participate in the Section's program of commissions because their work was not artistic enough.

While none of these personal characteristics makes Zorach more or less important, they do explain why she proceeded in developing her sketches as she did, how she found artifacts and animals to include in those sketches, and how she functioned within the Section's lockstep payment-for-progress formula. For example, she saw nothing wrong in asking for an extension on her Monticello contract because she had too much to do with her garden to devote the time needed to painting.

The Monticello commission was the last of the three she received, and she knew she would be questioned about the authenticity of her Indiana designs so she told Edward B. Rowan: "I am fortunate having a charming Finnish girl here this summer studying with Bill [her husband, a major sculptor] who is familiar with Monticello." Still she sent only two pencil sketches to Washington for consideration, one of a picnic scene and one of a haying scene, saying "everything is there except what's in my head," meaning they were rough sketches.

> I would enjoy doing either one. It is all first hand material—(I don't like using secondhand material if I can avoid it). The hay is Zorach hay transferred to Indiana—but hay is curiously universal—the tree is ours and the people I just collect.
>
> I plan to have a lake in the background—Monticello likes its lake—and general Indiana farm land and farms. This is for both sketches.

Rowan liked both ideas but thought the "recumbent figures" in the picnic scene might lead to "local criticism" unless they were redesigned.

> There is a handsome, lyrical quality in the haying scene. The male figure in the foreground seems a little out of relation with the other two adult figures, but I'm sure that this could be corrected in the further progress of the work. . . . The horse in this design is very beautiful.

On 20 August 1941 the artist sent color sketches to Washington, the second step in the commissioning process and the one that had to precede any payment. She apologized for the pale quality of the watercolors, saying that she never could do one as strong as the oil painting would be.

> The yellow and black spotted pig is ours and he's a most attractive pig but if you think him too sporty or unusual I can change him for a plain pig. . . . Also I like the idea of looking up to the figure on the hay load and feeling him very high in the picture (as in life).

The actual mural space, she pointed out, was going to be a foot wider than the blueprint incorrectly indicated.

> I've always made my P. O. murals a lot larger than you asked for because I liked the space. And I particularly like this space so I really don't mind too much except that I haven't recovered yet from having to pay $50.00 for the canvas.

Someone in the Section office penciled a note on the side of the letter that eight hundred dollars was the amount allowed under the 1 percent agreement and "this project was set up for sculpture originally."

Nine months later, on 25 May 1942, Zorach asked for an extension of the contract. Part of her problem was the size of the mural itself. She lived in New York City most of the time, with a small studio. During the summers she and her family moved to a farm in Maine, where she had a studio large enough to handle the Monticello canvas and where she grew the hay and pigs she included in the mural. She had been ill, she told Rowan, and the spring had been too cold to paint much in Maine, "and now we have lots of gardens planted—acres—and can't get any help and it means dividing my time." Rowan could not offer much help:

> I regret to state that the administrative costs under which the Section of Fine Arts is operated have been greatly reduced and extensions of contracts can only be allowed for the most compelling reasons. The illness to which you refer would suffice, but I do want you to decide on the earliest possible date that you know the work could be completed and installed.

A few days later she replied that she could be finished by September, but she did not know how long it would take to get approval of the cartoon, set the date for installation, and take care of other details, such as the required photographs, which she had not sent at the halfway stage. Rowan asked for a photograph of the "cartoon or of half-completed stage as that is necessary for payment," and they could not get out of sync or she would never be paid.

On 28 July she sent word that "the mural is almost finished . . . I apologize for no photos." On 14 August she sent another note to Rowan. "I am sending photo of finished mural and hope the Section approves." Apparently, as the Section by then was already beginning to close up shop, Rowan was able to have her paid, even if things were "out of sync."

When the postmaster sent the official installation-completed letter, he included a somewhat tongue-in-cheek editorial from the *Monticello White County Democrat*:

> Since every person in Indiana is a poet and author, and presumably an art critic, the thing to do is to go to the postoffice and pass an opinion on the mural painting placed on the west wall. . . .
>
> We cannot make up our mind whether the scene is reminiscent of the past or prophetic of the future. It is in a pastoral vein, with the farmer knee deep in hay and the lazy river flowing along peacefully in the distance.
>
> But we do not know whether the horse drawn wagons and cart portray the period prior to the advent of motor vehicles, or whether the artist is suggesting a scene of rural life after tires are worn out and the consumption of gasoline is restricted. We do not know whether the hired man who is pitching the hay is getting 75 cents or $5.00 a day. We do not know whether the particular tool in the hands of the lady, probably used to turn over the hay, indicates the antiquity of the scene, or whether the tool has been resurrected due to the shortage of farm machinery.

Nevertheless, we think the painting puts color in the postoffice. There is action in the picture, and cheerfulness, and no matter how many times you look at the painting, there is always some new detail to observe. We think it adds something to the town.

Marguerite Zorach also painted *New Hampshire Post in Winter* for Peterborough, New Hampshire, in 1938 and *Autumn* for Ripley, Tennessee, in 1940.

W hen Grant Christian received the letter inviting him
to submit sketches for a post office mural, the location
was given as Bloomington, Illinois. For some reason,
probably a lack of funds at the last minute, no mural
was authorized for that location. Rather, Christian was told to visit
Nappanee to gather information there for a mural.

On 24 April 1937 the artist wrote to Edward B. Rowan that he had
completed the requisite visit:

> The Postmaster took me out in the country and introduced me to
> some of the leading farmers of the community and explained the
> process of distilling mint, which is an important industry in that
> part of the country. There is an Amish settlement in Nappanee and
> Mr. Troup [the postmaster] explained many of the characteristics
> of these interesting people.

Apparently Christian misunderstood the required process, for he
submitted a color sketch of the design he wished to pursue before
submitting several pencil sketches of different possibilities. In addition,

TITLE
Waiting for the Mail

SIZE
10'9" x 4'

ARTIST
Grant Christian

FEE
$520

BASIS FOR THE AWARD
*Competent design in Louisville,
Kentucky, competition*

MEDIUM
Oil on canvas

DATES
*Contract 6 October 1937 for
237 calendar days*
*Postmaster letter confirming
installation, 17 March 1938*

LOCATION OF BUILDING
202 East Market Street

the Section staff moved its offices and misplaced the artist's sketch. When the sketch was found, the Section's response was not positive:

> I regret to tell you that the members of the Section do not feel that you have submitted the best possible decoration for this space of which you are capable. . . . The main objection to your design is that it is too crowded and the treatment of the figures is too theatrical.

In September Christian sent four new pencil sketches to Washington, with a happier result.

> These, in our opinion, are a great improvement over the original designs submitted. The preferred design is that of the girl standing at the gate. It is handsomely drawn and unusual in subject matter. The large area of the fence, however, even though broken with shadow, might prove monotonous. What do you think of introducing some further object between the mail box and the tree: a dog for instance in profile with an attitude of waiting?

As the completed mural shows, Christian incorporated exactly that idea into the design, with a satisfactory result.

On 19 October the color sketch of the girl at the mailbox was approved. When the photograph of the half-completed mural was received, Rowan wrote that the photograph "indicates that the work has progressed satisfactorily." On 6 March 1938 Christian installed the mural, and on 17 March 1938 Postmaster Troup confirmed the installation met all expectations.

Why then did Christian write a long letter to Rowan on 4 September 1941 asking for another assignment, even in "some little old out of the way post office" at any time? To answer that question from the perspective of hindsight, one must go back to a brief Indianapolis newsstory when the Nappanee mural was installed:

> A second commission to do a post office mural came to Grant Christian from the Federal government as a result of the satisfaction over his handling the series of historic panels placed in the Indianapolis Federal building last December. Mr. Christian was in Nappanee over the week end to install a large horizontal panel, measuring 10 feet 9 inches in width and 4 feet in height, in the post office at that place.
>
> The subject matter, dealing with the rural delivery of mail, is handled simply. A young girl, at the center of interest in a setting of

> farm-home landscape, stands near the mailbox awaiting the arrival of the rural mail carrier.
>
> Young Christian is doing layout work for the Keeling & Co. Advertising Agency in the Chamber of Commerce building. He says that his steady job leaves him ample time in which to paint pictures.

In his 1941 letter Christian said that he had "entered most every mural competition that I was eligible to compete in and have enough mimeographed rejection slips to paper my walls." He wondered if his "subject matter or point of view" was "all wrong."

> I have studied what the juries accept and what the public usually looks for in painting. Perhaps the public is too factual or literary but they pay the bill so why should artists deliberately try to displease them?

Rowan circulated Christian's letter, along with photographs of his Nappanee and Indianapolis murals and competition entries, to the other members of the Section staff asking if they would suggest another commission. In the meantime he responded to Christian, and his reasoning boils down to a classic "Catch-22" situation: because Christian was so good at what he did for a living, he was not acceptable as a mural artist.

> My own reaction to your work since you seem to be interested in that is that it is possibly too illustrative and too artificially decorative. . . . The War Department competition sketch which you submitted carries more feeling for magazine illustration than for wall painting.

In other words, Christian was told that because he had to earn a living and because he did it as an illustrator and because he did it so well, his work was not acceptable. The artist becomes a victim of the necessity of the person to survive, to earn a living.

A November letter confirmed that the other staff members concurred with Rowan, who added one final comment dealing with the diminishing status of the Section:

Due to the limited number of mural reservations available due to the emergency, the Section has adopted the policy of reserving commissions only for runners up in competitions.

Ironically, Christian's Nappanee mural remains one of the most popular in the Indiana group of post office murals. When World War II came, four years after the mural was installed, *Waiting for the Mail* took on a new meaning—waiting for the mail from "overseas." In a 1975 interview the postmaster said the residents gave a new interpretation to the painting; even though the flag is still up on the mailbox—meaning the carrier has not arrived—many Nappanee patrons said the mural showed a time when the mail carrier had already come, and there still was no word from loved ones at war.

In 1935 and 1936, before receiving the commission for the Nappanee mural, Grant Christian supervised for the Treasury Relief Art Project (TRAP) the series of panels in the downtown Indianapolis federal building showing *Early and Present Day Indianapolis Life* and *Mail—Transportation and Delivery.*

TITLE
*Indiana Farm—Sunday
Afternoon*

SIZE
9'6" x 4'

ARTIST
Alan Tompkins

FEE
$540

BASIS FOR THE AWARD
*"Competent work executed
under the Treasury Department
Art Projects"*

MEDIUM
Oil on canvas

DATES
*Contract 20 January 1938 for
131 calendar days*

*Letter confirming installation, 20
June 1938*

LOCATION OF BUILDING
202 East Third Street

In one of his letters to the Section, Alan Tompkins mentions a major problem faced by the muralists, how to fit the mural into the predetermined space without impeding upon the architectural integrity of the building and without seeming to compete with the posters and announcements already on display in the lobby. In an 8 January 1938 letter to Edward B. Rowan in the Section, Tompkins highlights another problem, the physical arrangement of the lobby:

> The total width of the room is only 11 feet, 5 inches. Also there is a vestibule projecting into the room only 8 feet from the wall to be decorated. . . .
>
> In my designs I have tried to use a panel small enough to be seen in its entirety from a distance of 15 feet and at the same time to use plenty of plain surfaces in the pictures which will relieve the unpleasant feeling of crowdedness I felt when I visited the post office.
>
> The sketches are misleading insofar as they show the bulletin board as plain surfaces, whereas they are most frequently a conglomeration of notices of all sizes not only filling the boards themselves but also tacked to the frames.

Since a long view of the whole panel is impossible, I have tried to keep my centers of interest low in the picture space.

In a 1978 interview the artist elaborated on his concerns with competing with other material in the lobby, saying the mural should "not attempt to outshout, for instance, the posters in the lobby, [which] very often are meant to be attention getters, Uncle Sam pointing his finger at you, etc. The mural certainly shouldn't be in that category."

Tompkins, who was "a teacher of still-life painting and composition and . . . lecturer on pictorial art" at the John Herron Art Institute from 1934 to 1938, fared better than many artists in terms of the comments from the Washington office about his designs. For North Manchester he submitted only two designs, both based upon a late afternoon in the summer.

As far as the subject matter is concerned, I have been influenced by the feeling of informality in the post office building itself and the impression of quiet rural calm in the town of North Manchester. In acknowledgment of the existence of Manchester College I have shown persons of college age in both the designs submitted.

Tompkins's preference was for the pencil sketch he called "Return from Work," but the Section liked "Indiana Farm—Sunday Afternoon" better and asked him to prepare the color sketch from that design.

On 2 March Rowan wrote that a "question was also raised as to whether the farmer's wife would be doing a family washing on Sunday." A week later Tompkins replied:

I have . . . changed her occupation to that of putting a pudding dish in the oven for Sunday night supper. I think this change will be equally successful as design and that it will clear up the inconsistency of subject I had not noticed.

A week after the artist's change in the duties of the farm wife, Rowan requested additional work on the faces:

Further attention is needed in the facial type which you have used. The face of the young girl could be made less insipid and the other faces treated in a somewhat more pleasant manner. They are rather uninteresting at present and slightly forbidding.

Finally, on 5 May after the artist submitted the photograph of the half-finished mural, Rowan expressed other concerns:

It is felt now that the head of the young woman needs further study as she seems insipidly pleasant. It will be appreciated if you will devote further study of this head in an effort to present her as a more natural and less affected type.

What should be noted in all these letters is the terminology used by Rowan in his criticisms: "question was raised," "further attention is needed," and "it will be appreciated if you will devote further study." None of the overtones of these terms is demanding or threatening, as occasionally occurred in other letters, perhaps because Tompkins needed make only minor changes to bring the design to culmination, as opposed to major changes needed in some works to bring them up to minimal acceptance.

In his 1978 interview Tompkins certainly did not recall the Section as being overpowering. When asked if he remembered Washington suggesting changes in any of his murals, he replied negatively:

I remember that they did not. There were no specific suggestions of changes. They wrote a letter commenting upon various facets of it. In one they kind of raved about the color. They might make a complimentary remark which tended to show you what it was they liked about it, and sometimes by omission you could assume that there were sides of it that they hoped you would improve. But it was as subtle as that. There were no directions, no orders.

The *Indianapolis Sunday Star* on 5 June 1938 carried a long feature article on Tompkins and the North Manchester mural. The writer, Lucille E. Morehouse, lauded the artist and the design:

Give me a large mural painting as the best means of becoming well acquainted with an artist's work and, incidentally, with the artist himself. In these days when the Federal government is generously giving out commissions to artists all over the country in order that the new post offices may have their walls artistically decorated, there is a tendency, on the part of some, to slight their work. Many pictures have been painted that are as lacking in imaginative feeling and the true creative art spirit as are the hundreds of "doughboy" statues that were erected after the World War.

The more forceful an artist's character, I have found, the more pains he has taken to put his very best into his designing and executing the commissions from the United States government. And certainly there must be more fun in making a picture in which imagination plays a large part than in doing a mere commercial stunt. I like Alan Tompkins's design and I like the way in which it is painted. He has not caricatured the farm folk. But he has interpreted the plain honesty and sturdiness of the type with sincerity of purpose and feeling.

That same article mentioned that Tompkins was leaving Indianapolis. As he told Rowan in a 7 June 1938 letter: "I am severing my connections with the John Herron Art School . . . and intend to return to my native environment, Connecticut or New York, to devote my entire time to painting."

His Martinsville mural, *The Arrival of the Mail,* was installed in 1937; he completed *Daniel Boone on a Hunting Trip in Watauga County* for Boone, North Carolina, in 1940; and he returned to Indianapolis for the installation of *Suburban Street* in the Indianapolis Broad Ripple station in 1942.

I n late 1937 Tom Rost, a native of Richmond, Indiana, then living in Milwaukee, received a commission from the Section of Fine Arts to prepare a mural for the Elkhorn, Wisconsin, post office lobby. While doing the suggested research with the postmaster, Rost became intrigued with the history of mail delivery begun in 1838 to this southern Wisconsin town and handled by a single traveler who made a weekly trip from Spring Prairie with the mail in his pockets and in his hat. Rost's mural, installed in early 1938, depicts such a postman taking letters from his hat for distribution to the waiting settlers.

When Edward B. Rowan wrote to Rost on 20 August 1938 inviting him to submit sketches for another mural, this time in Paoli, Indiana, Rost decided to pursue the mail delivery theme again. He sent three sketches to Washington for the Section members to review. The first one depicted one of the two stagecoaches used to carry mail "to and from New Albany, on the Ohio River, until 1912. The Orange County Court House is in the background." In sketch number two the artist

TITLE
Rural Mail Carrier

SIZE
12' x 5'3"

ARTIST
Tom Rost

FEE
$670

BASIS FOR THE AWARD
"Competent work performed under the Treasury Department Art Projects"

MEDIUM
Oil on canvas

DATES
Contract 4 January 1939, number of days not specified

Postmaster letter confirming installation, 28 June 1939

LOCATION OF BUILDING
202 North Gospel Street

put the same stage in the hills surrounding the town. "The folks in this part of Indiana are proud of their fine, large orchards and poultry farms which are suggested in this sketch." Rost mentioned to Rowan in the 11 January 1939 letter that accompanied the sketches that he had met "the old driver of the stage coach," who was now driving "the town taxicab."

According to a newspaper article in the *Indianapolis Star* on 22 June 1939, shortly after the mural was installed, that while in Paoli to research the town and its industries and history, Rost was "impressed with an old photograph of the first three rural mail carriers working out of Paoli, along with their mail wagons or square-topped buggies, such as were used for the first rural delivery." A "narrow-bed wagon which the rural carriers drove out of Paoli until 1918" appears in Rost's third sketch sent to Washington. Again "the orchards and chickens appear," this time with a farm family. This is the sketch the Section approved for development.

Even though the artist chose another historical setting for his Indiana mural, "1902, when the first rural free delivery was made," what separates this work from his earlier mural in Wisconsin is the background setting, described in detail by the newspaper writer:

> The mural covers the entire wall space above the door on one side of the lobby. In it appears the Orange county Courthouse, built in 1856, the tall spire of the Friends Church, some of the taller buildings on the public square, the farmland of the surrounding country side and the industries and products of this city.

So well did the artist do his job that even today visitors to the lobby will say they know the spot where the artist stood to compose the background for the mural, yet the buildings shown could not be seen in that perspective and in that relationship from any one spot; rather it is a composite of several vantage points, a creation of the imagination of the artist.

In addition to *Pioneer Postman* for Elkhorn, Wisconsin, in 1938, Rost painted *Farm Yard* for Lancaster, Wisconsin, in 1940.

TITLE
Loggers

SIZE
12' x 5'

ARTIST
William F. Kaeser

FEE
$560

BASIS FOR THE AWARD
Runner-up in Jasper, Indiana/East Detroit, Michigan, competition

MEDIUM
Oil on canvas

DATES
Contract 15 February 1939 for 258 days

Postmaster letter confirming installation, 13 December 1939

LOCATION OF BUILDING
137 State Street

William F. Kaeser came to the United States from Germany in 1923 at age fifteen. After graduating from high school he studied at the Leonardo da Vinci Art School in New York City before entering the John Herron Art Institute in Indianapolis in 1928. He graduated in 1932 in the depths of the depression. In a 1978 interview he described the conditions:

> The reason I went to Indiana University is that I graduated from Herron in '32, and you couldn't get a job under any circumstances— could work at Ayres, in sales, you know—but you couldn't get a job [in an art related field].

He still had a studio downtown when an acquaintance saw the drawings Kaeser had done at Herron.

> He saw all these life-sized nude drawings I made in school . . . life-sized charcoal drawings, and he came up with an idea. He put them around a lampshade, and a lot of the young people would buy them. The girls would buy the fellows, and the fellows would buy the

girls. And he sold all those drawings for me. . . . I got enough money to go to school at IU; that's how I got the money, selling those pictures that summer.

I decided I'd go to IU and get my teacher's license in Art and German. . . . I finished it all in one year. And still couldn't get a job.

What came next is an important element in the history of art in Indianapolis, the indirect creation of the group that became the Indianapolis Art League. When no teaching jobs were available Kaeser checked out the opportunities the WPA Art Projects offered unemployed artists. Because of his training and skills he was hired to teach art to a class he gathered together. "We had an open house. I called it the Art Students League at that time, after New York. I thought, 'Let the students decide who their teacher should be.' That's the art league philosophy in New York and that's what I thought [would work] here."

When his contract for the Pendleton mural was signed, Kaeser discovered he no longer qualified for assistance under the WPA program. That is, with "regular" employment as an artist he was ineligible for WPA employment, and he had to cancel the art classes he was teaching. "While it wasn't much money," he later commented, "at that time it was like a fortune."

Because he no longer qualified for WPA employment as an instructor, ten of his students began to pay him directly to teach them. "You see, to be a student in an art class . . . you have to buy paints and canvases and you have to have money, and you couldn't be a poor student because they [WPA] weren't furnishing any materials." According to Kaeser, that group of students ultimately became the Indianapolis Art League.

When Kaeser qualified as a runner-up in the regional competition for post office murals in Jasper and in East Detroit, the Section invited him to submit sketches for a Pendleton mural. As Pendleton was only twenty-five or so miles from the artist's home, he visited the city for ideas.

I did one of the train coming by and picking up the mail. I figured that's kind of interesting. Then I did [the loggers] because logging was an important thing in the early history; there was a lot of woods. The Postmaster also wanted the swimming hole they have over there. Then I did one of that grain elevator. That was the thing that was really interesting. I thought it was an interesting structure with the railroad and a wagon coming in with corn and unloading. [The Postmaster] said, "I'm not going to advertise that guy's grain elevator." I thought it made a terrific composition.

He sent four sketches to Washington: hauling grain to the elevator, loggers, building the levee, and receipt of the mail.

The Section staff liked at least three of the four, finding value in each of them. "The one entitled 'Loggers' occurs to us to be the most unusual in subject matter and treatment and if this subject matter is related to the locale this is the design we would like you to carry out in a two-inch scale color sketch." At the same time, "Hauling Grain" looked good, too, while " 'Building the Levee' has much more dramatic quality in it and in the end would no doubt prove a more satisfactory design."

Finally Edward B. Rowan told Kaeser in a 16 February 1939 letter to take all the sketches to the postmaster "and have him advise with you relative to the one containing the most appropriate subject matter for that building." That was a worthwhile piece of advice since a few weeks later the postmaster wrote the Section asking if "this office will have any choice in the Art work to be done." Rowan told him "any suggestions . . . will be greatly appreciated, I am sure, by the artist." A few days later Kaeser visited Pendleton again and was able to tell Rowan in an 11 March letter that the postmaster seemed very pleased with the sketches and "agreed with the opinion of your committee that the one entitled 'Loggers' is the most appropriate design for the purpose."

After all that agreement by all parties concerned about the value of the logging design, the Section staff made few critical comments as Kaeser proceeded with the mural. At one point they felt "the tones of the horses and foreground tend to be disturbingly low for a mural painting. It is our experience that an oil painting keyed as low as this is difficult to be seen once it is installed on the wall." Kaeser remembered that they felt the figures were "a little small." He wanted the horses to look powerful, so he diminished the figures of the two men, but finally made them larger at the Section's suggestion. "You see, you got criticism [from the Section] that if you just did it on your own, you would probably overlook."

On 12 December 1939 Rowan wrote to Kaeser about another of his sketches:

I am happy to tell you that the design of the "Workers" which you submitted in the forty-eight state mural competition was well liked by Mr. Bruce and several others and at the present time is being exhibited in the Gallery of the Section of Fine Arts. With your permission we would like to retain it for a while longer for exhibition purposes.

Within a few months William Kaeser entered the army. He painted no other post office murals.

About the time John E. Costigan completed his mural, *Workers of the Soil,* for Girard, Ohio, in 1938, he received a letter from Edward B. Rowan asking him to submit drawings for a possible mural commission in Rensselaer, Indiana. That possibility became a reality, and Costigan's *Receiving the Mail on the Farm* was installed in 1939. Three years later he installed another *Receiving the Mail on the Farm,* this time in Stuart, Virginia.

One observer looked at black and white photographs of the three murals and thought they represented three stages of the same mural, probably as the artist worked from color sketch to cartoon to completed canvas, not three separate murals. Perhaps Costigan should have called his Ohio work "Farm Theme," his Indiana mural "Variation on a Theme #1," and his Virginia mural "Variation on a Theme #2," for the three murals contain identical figures, identical groupings of figures, and identical themes; the only changes come in the placement of those elements in the designs. No other artist with multiple commissions repeated or was allowed to repeat the same scheme over and over. Perhaps he was indulged because Rowan saw a "simple spiritual quality" in the mural, and although the Section disallowed woodland nymphs and gauze-covered maidens in its post office murals, even

TITLE
Receiving the Mail on the Farm

SIZE
12' x 4'

ARTIST
John E. Costigan

FEE
$670

BASIS FOR THE AWARD
Designs submitted in Interior Department competition

MEDIUM
Oil on canvas

DATES
Contract 15 September 1938 for 166 calendar days

Postmaster letter confirming installation, 28 February 1939

LOCATION OF BUILDING
225 South Van Rensselaer Street

it could not turn down a variation on the classical "Madonna and Child" motif.

> Your designs have been considered by the members of the Section and the Supervising Architect and I am pleased to tell you that the design which you have labeled Number 1, showing the family group of a mother and father and three children, is the preferred design. This is very handsome in its implications, solid in structure and most appealing in its rhythmic qualities. We are confident that you will create a beautiful mural with this design.

Later in this 14 September 1938 letter Rowan refers to a statement from the postmaster in Girard, Ohio, that the first mural had been installed, so Rowan was aware from the beginning of the similarities between the 1938 Ohio mural and the 1939 Indiana work.

By November, with the receipt of the photograph of the full-size cartoon, Rowan could spell out the "handsome implications" in the design. "I discussed it with the Supervising Architect this morning and I know you will be pleased to hear that he pronounced it a serious work of great weight and beauty. And truly it has the quality of a holy picture." When Costigan later sent the photograph of the mural installed in the lobby, Rowan again spoke of the ethereal nature of the project:

> I want to congratulate you on the consummate quality of this mural. I am confident that no one visiting the Post Office in Rensselaer can see it without being affected by the simple spiritual quality which pervades the work. . . .
>
> Relative to the photographs, I am really disturbed that they do not do your work greater justice as we should like to reproduce your mural in various publications but the photographs which you submitted are not sufficient for that. Is there any way that you could supply us with an excellent photograph and negative of this painting?

Costigan must be given some credit here, for he never once made any reference to "holy" qualities in his designs. In fact the only element he wished to aggrandize was the work of "the Post Office Department . . . in bringing happiness and knowledge to the people who live far from the large cities."

Costigan had lived in the largest of American cities, New York City, from 1903 to 1918, having moved there from Providence, Rhode Island, at age fifteen to work in a lithographer's shop, where for a number of years he "did lettering" during the day and went to class at night.

> I did not study under any man, am self-taught. The Kit Kat Club in N. Y. City ran a class 5 nights a week; there was no instructor. One painted or drew what ever they wished; most of the members were commercial men who worked during the day and went to the club at night to paint. I hardly missed a night in 8 or 10 years and that is where most of my study was.

Following nine months in France during World War I, Costigan moved in 1919 to Orangeburg, New York, a small town just north of New York City and west of the Hudson River. Between then and 1938, when he sent this biographical sketch to Forbes Watson, his oil paintings had been selected for the permanent collections of the Art Institute of Chicago, the Metropolitan Museum, the Duncan Phillips Memorial Gallery in Washington, D.C., the Montclair, New Jersey, Museum, and the New Orleans Museum.

O pen almost any textbook devoted to twentieth-century American art to look for the names of the artists who painted the murals in the Indiana post offices, and the one most apt to be found is Milton Avery, indicating his artistic stature during the decade of the 1930s. Yet no mural produced by any other artist in Indiana caused both the Section and the artist so much grief before it was attached to the lobby wall. The problem came from the fact that Avery is known as an early Abstract painter; the Section press release for the Rockville mural notes "his understanding of the use of simple masses in design." Even though his work does not resemble that of the Abstract Expressionists to come in the 1950s, he certainly was no American Scene painter.

His invitation to submit sketches came from one obvious source, his entry in the Interior Department competition, and one less public source, an early painting of his. When Avery submitted his first Rockville sketches to Washington, Edward B. Rowan wrote to Avery on 4 October 1938:

> Of the four designs the one which I have marked for you is preferred. It is a simple landscape with an apple tree in the foreground. It is charming in its present implications and in order to enliven the composition for the larger scale, you might introduce a calf or colt

TITLE
Landscape

SIZE
12' x 4'

ARTIST
Milton Avery

FEE
$670

BASIS FOR THE AWARD
"Design submitted in Interior Department Competition"

MEDIUM
Oil on canvas

DATES
Contract 1 October 1938 for 181 calendar days

Postmaster letter confirming installation, 16 August 1939

LOCATION OF BUILDING
Corner of Ohio and Market Streets

in the foreground on the left. I remember with such appreciation your lyric painting with a calf in the foreground on exhibition at The Little Gallery, Cedar Rapids, Iowa.

Ironically, Rowan's remembrance of the calf and offhanded suggestion led Avery to try to incorporate these animals in his landscape, always with increasingly less satisfaction on everyone's part.

When the artist sent a photograph of the full-sized cartoon in December, the Section staff found his approach "too obviously naive," meaning that apparently the design was too simple for a mural painting, although it would be "perfectly appropriate for an easel painting." Rowan then suggested "further study be given to the drawing of the trees and the calf."

A few days later Avery sent another photograph of a more detailed version of the cartoon, saying that he felt it would be "much more spacious without the calf in the foreground." One of the Section staff penciled a note beside this comment: "He would not be kidding us would he?" A hint of additional trouble to come can be found in the artist's comment about detailed drawings. "I realize now that you would like to see a detailed drawing of the mural, but that is not my particular way of working. I like to develop a painting with pigment as I go along."

Development as one works may be appropriate when one works on one's own time and money, but when working for an exacting patron, such as Rowan and the Section staff, realistic details are necessary. On 27 December 1938 Rowan again wrote to Avery, informing him of their dissatisfaction with his lack of sensitivity to his intended audience:

> It does not occur to me that you are taking into consideration the fact that you are painting a mural for a non-painting public. The sophisticated naivete which you have brought to bear on the design is one which I am convinced will not be understood or readily received by the citizens of Rockville. Can you not introduce into this design some of the joy and delight in landscape that you had in the painting of a calf which I once showed in The Little Gallery and of which I wrote you several times?

The most devastating comment for a financially struggling artist came next: "I am withholding the voucher covering the payment due you at this stage until I have your reaction to the suggestions of this letter."

Eventually Rowan realized that if anything was to come from this effort Avery would have to be allowed to work his own way, and approval was given to begin painting the actual mural, without a detailed cartoon. When the artist submitted the required "progress" photo at

the halfway stage, the Section staff noted a more satisfactory development of the canvas "than the cartoon indicated," but realism was still lacking. Rowan was not convinced that the animal he saw in the foreground was a cow:

> [S]ince this is the only element in your composition which requires careful drawing, it is suggested that you re-study the animal, introducing the conviction of personal observation in this. The mural is going into a community where it will be seen by a great many farmers and this is the first thing that many of them would pounce on to criticize.
>
> Frankly, your whole design would be improved if you could create the conviction of authentic observation throughout.

In other words, go look at a cow and at the Indiana landscape around Rockville.

This whole exchange must have been doubly frustrating for Rowan. After all, he had suggested the cow in the first place because he had seen a realistic cow in the earlier painting, yet now the artist could not produce even this one authentic element correctly.

In March Forbes Watson visited Avery's studio and family, with whom he viewed the completed mural, "which, to put it mildly, is something," as he confided in his report:

> It was quite a heartrending hour that I spent with them. I asked Mr. Avery if he had ever been in Indiana, and he said that he had not. Since the mural is for the Rockville, Indiana Post Office, and since it is entirely a landscape subject, I explained as gently as I could, with clarity, that I couldn't help feeling that the landscape which he

had painted had so little of the character of the place that I doubted if it would be a satisfactory mural.

On 6 April 1939 Rowan wrote to Avery with the dolorous news that the acting supervising architect of the Public Buildings Administration would not approve the mural for installation because it "does not convincingly reflect the locale of the building in which it is to be placed." Rowan picked up on Watson's concern about the authenticity of the landscape, saying that the painting "appears to reflect your visits to Vermont more than an acquaintance with the landscape in and around Rockville." Even the trees lacked genuineness and the "vitality and conviction that could only be gained through a study of such a tree in nature. It is not in any way that we wish you to photographically reproduce a tree; it is just that the form is not pleasing or convincing to us." Rowan was so desperate that he had checked out Rockville to discover its "leading industries are lumber, shale and clay, flour mill, agriculture and live stock." If Avery would just put some realistic livestock, certified by the postmaster to be "abundant in that region," in the foreground of the painting and perhaps in one or two of the meadows in the landscape, the "foreground material will keep [the people of Rockville] from objecting too strenuously to the discrepancies in the landscape."

Even though another visitor to the artist's studio suggested the simplest solution to the problem was to pay him off and forget the mural, and even though the artist himself finally protested that the painting in The Little Gallery to which Rowan kept referring "was primarily a cow picture with the landscape as a background," as opposed to this landscape with cows, Rowan persisted in his suggestions, criticisms, and encouragements.

Finally in early July the Rockville mural was installed, and in August the postmaster confirmed its acceptability. In what must be a classic example of circumlocution, the Section of Fine Arts press release lauds the artist's "unusual feeling for color and his understanding of the use of simple masses in design."

> Like the landscapes of many of his contemporaries, the rural scene, which is the subject of this artist's mural, is not a picture of a specific place. On the contrary, Mr. Avery has concentrated the results of many landscape studies in a single composition through which he interprets his feeling for Indiana country.

Needless to say, Milton Avery received no further commissions for post office murals.

TITLE
Harvesting

SIZE
14' x 5'

ARTIST
Joseph Meert

FEE
$720

BASIS FOR THE AWARD
48-State Mural Competition winner

MEDIUM
Tempera and oil on canvas

DATES
Contract 15 January 1940 for 366 calendar days

Postmaster letter confirming installation, 6 August 1940

LOCATION OF BUILDING
30 South Washington Street

I n the brief history of the Section of Fine Arts, no competition brought as many qualified designs or fostered more controversy than the 48-State Mural Competition held in 1939.

One post office in each state was chosen for decoration and its location and dimensions were announced in the Section's *Bulletin* that went to 6,500 artists, writers, and teachers—almost everyone associated with the visual arts in the United States. Unlike most other Section competitions, artists were not required to live in or be "attached to" a particular state in order to submit designs for an earmarked location.

As this was a national competition, the Section selected nationally recognized judges to make the choices: Maurice Sterne, Olin Dows, Edgar Miller, and Henry Varnum Poor, all highly qualified for their task. They interpreted their charge from the Section as the responsibility to choose not just the best design for a specific town from those submitted for that town but from all 1,476 designs submitted for all towns. In retrospect, that must have been a truly mind-boggling assignment, and when *Life* magazine published small photographs of the jury's choices for all forty-eight towns and cities, the resulting outcry surely must have made the panel wonder if they would have been better off to have said "No" when asked to serve in the first place.

Two different responses to the choices appeared in letters to the Section, to the editors of dozens of newspapers across the country, and in numerous editorials. The first response, the one the Section hoped for of course, was one that applauded the choice of artist and design as appropriate to the location and the local perspective on history or industrial development. Usually this response came when the design chosen by the jury was one that had been submitted for that exact post office. The second response came when the jury recommended an artist be given a commission for a post office other than the one the design was intended for, whether another building in the same state or the location chosen by the Section for the competition, but in a different state.

The former response came with the design submitted by Avery Johnson (who painted the Liberty, Indiana, mural) for the Bordentown, New Jersey, site; the judges liked his design, and he was awarded the commission. The latter response came with the work of two other artists who painted in Indiana: Alan Tompkins and Joseph Meert.

Tompkins, who lived in Connecticut, submitted a design for the East Hartford post office; the design portrayed a shade-grown tobacco crop appropriate to this northern state. The jury chose Tompkins's design but awarded him the commission for the Boone, North Carolina, post office. The local residents protested that his design had nothing to do with the tobacco crops of North Carolina. He made a radical change in his design, from tobacco to *Daniel Boone on a Hunting Trip in Watauga County.*

Joseph Meert, who lived in Kansas City, Missouri, submitted a wheat harvesting design for the post office in Seneca, Kansas. The judges liked his design but liked someone else's better for the Kansas location. The solution—give a commission to Meert but for the building in Spencer, Indiana, because none of the designs submitted specifically for Spencer met the standards of the judges. The judges never intended for these changed-location choices to be completed without appropriate, local modifications, but when the pictures of the selected murals began appearing in local newspapers and in the *Life* story, no one seemed to realize changes could be and would be made by the artists, if necessary.

Within days of the appearance of the magazine story, Ben Kaufman, editor and publisher of the *Spencer Evening World,* wrote to Meert. "It so happens that Owen County, of which Spencer is the county seat, is more of a corn-raising country than of wheat." To support his claims

Kaufman checked with the county agent, who confirmed the "corn crop is from four to five times as large as the wheat crop." Not only did the local critic object to the crops Meert presented, he also questioned the artist's landscape: "Also you will be interested to know the country here is hilly and there is little level, rolling land for farming." The rest of the design met with the editor's approval:

> Your mural shows in the distance something that could be a mine tipple. Is that what you intend for it to be? This would be appropriate since there is coal mining in Owen County. Also limestone quarrying.
>
> Chief industries here are a large printing plant . . . a clothes pin factory and a large pharmaceutical house.
>
> The train in the distance is also fine, since there are train lines through the country, hauling coal, limestone and other freight.

For Meert, incorporating such truth to location would be no problem; in fact, his teachers at the Art Students League in New York City had included some of the finest Realist painters in the country: John Sloan, Kenneth H. Miller, Boardman Robinson, and Thomas Hart Benton, best known to Hoosiers for his large 1933 Chicago World's Fair murals for the Indiana Pavilion. The changes were included without problem and without fanfare; in fact, there were few extreme changes in Meert's view, as he told Rowan in a 21 May 1940 letter, probably sent at the time the artist submitted the required photograph of the full-sized cartoon:

> You will note that the center is the only part which has been drastically changed. Since corn is the chief crop grown in the neighborhood of Spencer, I have there depicted a field of young corn. The wheat harvest which originally appeared at the left of the panel has been changed to hay, since this crop is found in any section of the country. The hills have been raised to suggest a more rugged country.

Joseph Meert also painted *Contemporary Life in Missouri* for Marceline, Missouri, in 1938 and *Spring Pastoral* for Mount Vernon, Missouri, in 1940.

TITLE
Indiana Farming

SIZE
12' x 7'

ARTIST
Donald M. Mattison

FEE
$700

BASIS FOR THE AWARD
Sketch for Rochester, Minnesota, competition

MEDIUM
Oil on canvas

DATES
Contract 10 May 1936 for 540 calendar days

Postmaster letter confirming installation, 3 March 1937

LOCATION OF BUILDING
203 East Jefferson Street

On 12 October 1937, seven months after his mural was installed on the lobby wall of the Tipton post office, Donald M. Mattison wrote his last letter about the mural to Forbes Watson, the Section adviser charged with gathering information about the narratives portrayed in all the murals, information which would be used in preparing the official press releases. The last sentence of the artist's letter provides an insightful clue to why this mural took almost one full calendar year to be completed. Mattison wrote Watson: "It was my ambition to express mood and significance of weather to the farmer." That simple yet difficult idea led the artist through three complete designs before he—not the officials in Washington—found the most appropriate one.

Mattison was director of the School of the John Herron Art Institute in Indianapolis when he submitted sketches in late 1935 for a mural design competition in Rochester, Minnesota. Although he did not win that competition, his sketch indicated he was worthy of an invitation to prepare possible designs for another building, this time in Tipton, and on 5 March 1936 Edward B. Rowan sent such a letter.

At this point in the story of the Tipton mural the files in the National Archives become sketchy and bear no record of correspondence again until 11 December 1936, when Rowan sent a somewhat negative commentary about Mattison's full-sized cartoon of a proposed mural called "A Prayer for Rain." Rowan criticized the overly dramatic poses of a few of the figures and suggested presenting them "in a more matter-of-fact way." He also disliked the representation of the sun:

Further, there is one feature in the treatment of the sky which is an affectation resulting from training in a particular school. I refer to the sunburst. This of course is a phenomenon that one occasionally sees, but I personally feel it has been overdone in mural painting.

Six days later Rowan wrote again, apparently not realizing that he had already made the same comments to Mattison in the earlier letter:

The design contains much of interest but the posture of most of the figures tends to be over-dramatic with little or no indication of the cause or purpose of such drama. I can understand that the theme has been conceived as a kind of festival, but would the scene not be as impressive and the mural as convincing if the figures were presented in a more matter of fact way?

The treatment of the sun bursting through the sky tends to add to the affectation of your approach. This, of course, is a phenomenon which one occasionally sees, but I personally feel that it has been over done in mural painting.

Even though Rowan added soothing words in both letters—"I am desirous only of being of some help to you" and "these criticisms may sound severe at first reading, but they are offered in a spirit of cooperation"—the back-to-back verbal assault was enough for Mattison.

Three weeks later, on 4 January 1937, the artist sent an entirely new sketch to Washington, a subject treated "in a matter-of-fact way as you have suggested—a subject which is more quickly understandable I hope." He added that the subject of the previous full-sized cartoon was "a 'Prayer for Rain' and to me one requiring a certain drama in treatment—poses, light, color and dramatic cloud effects. I find it hard to visualize the same composition in any other way." Almost as an aside Mattison added that this design, which actually is the third one he submitted and the one which occupies the wall today, "seems to me to be a better one for the space as well." He closed the letter with yet another apology: "I have caused you I'm afraid undue trouble in switching around so much but please put it down to my real desire to do the best of which I am capable."

Even the Washington officials knew that Mattison's efforts went above and beyond that usually expected, and Rowan's somewhat chagrined response—"I was very much amazed to have you forward us a third design in color for the mural"—went to Mattison in a 9 January letter:

The second design is acceptable to us and if you have proceeded as far as the full-sized cartoon [which, in fact he had done] it was not my intention so grossly to interfere with your work but merely to call your attention to certain reactions which we had toward the over-dramatic in the mural with the hope that in the painting you would alleviate this somewhat.

Your last design [that is, the one just received in the Washington office] is acceptable to us as were the first and second and certainly we wish you to carry out the one which interests you the most and which in your opinion represents your best efforts. At this distance our tendency is to advise you to proceed with the full-sized cartoon of design #2 but you understand, of course, that there is no coercion in this.

Few artists were given that kind of carte blanche by Rowan, and the contemporary viewer today only can wonder why Mattison chose to stick with the third design, to which he gave the generic *Indiana Farming* title, rather than his proposed "A Prayer for Rain." Perhaps it was a kind of artistic insight that led him to complete his story of "a Hoosier farm scene at a moment when a storm threatens in the early evening," because when completed, it certainly brought an appreciative recognition from the viewers.

While installing the canvas I particularly noticed that the post office was used for the greater part by people connected with farming and was pleased with the remarks especially of one man who said that he had washed his face every day for thirty years at a table placed outside his kitchen door and had often ridden a horse in from the fields in just such a way as the man in the mural. I did want just such people as he is to get something from the painting.

The artist's "ambition to express mood and significance of weather to the farmer" was achieved in Tipton, Indiana.

Donald M. Mattison also painted *Country Cousins* for Union City in 1938.

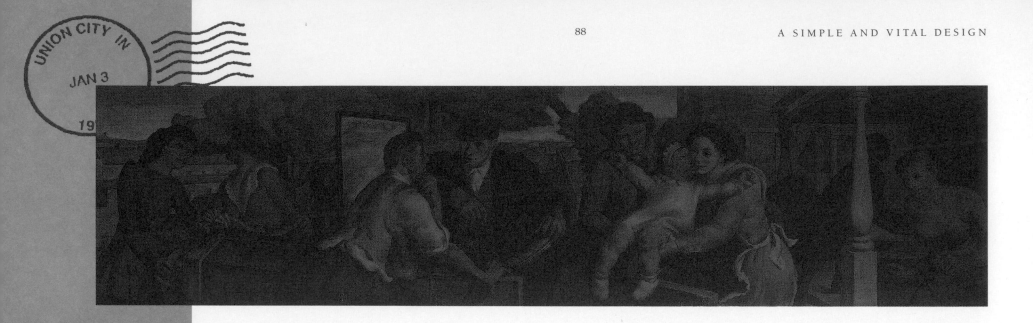

UNION CITY IN
JAN 3
19

TITLE
Country Cousins

SIZE
12' x 3'

ARTIST
Donald M. Mattison

FEE
$570

BASIS FOR THE AWARD
*"Competent work executed
under the Treasury Department
Art Projects"*

MEDIUM
Oil on canvas

DATES
*Contract 3 January 1938 for
148 calendar days*

*Postmaster letter confirming
installation, 6 May 1938*

LOCATION OF BUILDING
102 Pearl Street

Nineteen thirty-eight was a "boom year" for Indiana art and artists. Twelve murals were installed in Hoosier post office lobbies that year, more than any other single year, and six of them were done by artists associated with the John Herron Art Institute in Indianapolis. During this period Joe Cox, who had studied at Herron, installed his railroad mural in Garrett; Henrik Martin Mayer, assistant director of the school, installed his Aurora ferry mural; Herron student Jessie Hull Mayer's mural of mail delivery was affixed to the wall in Culver; Raymond L. Morris, who studied for a while at the school, finished his portrayal of the evening mail stagecoach for Knightstown; Alan Tompkins, who had taught for four years at Herron before returning to Yale as an instructor, finished his second Indiana mural, this one for North Manchester; and Donald M. Mattison, director of the school, completed the Union City mural.

Of the twelve murals attached to the walls that year, half represented historic themes—arrival of settlers and town founders—while the other half fall into the Regionalist genre, that catchall category of midwestern values and locations so beloved by the critics and patrons of the 1930s.

The two central groupings of the Union City painting—the two adult males on the left and the two females and baby on the right—symbolize the concerns and hopes of the current day and of the future. The man facing the viewer, who has just driven in from the country, has made a sober comment to his listener, who has put his hand to his chin in contemplation. Since the trees seem to be in full bloom, the visitor—the country cousin—may be talking about how the crops look for the fall, or what the prices of corn or wheat or hogs will be at harvesttime. Even today the spectator can applaud the speaker's frugality in time of economic hardship. The painting was done in 1938, but the car in the mural certainly is no racy, new Chrysler Zephyr with aerodynamic design or a magnificent Cord or Duesenberg; rather it represents a Model T-type vehicle, solid, safe, reliable, just like its owner. On the right the women and baby depict family values, home, and the future. By 1938 the depression still controlled much of the economic path of the country, but this family says that it will believe in the future and will bring children into the society.

On the far left we can hypothesize that the teenage girl on the bike has seen the arrival of her cousin and has come racing home from downtown or from a neighbor's house; immediately the two girls are exchanging stories, gossip, and dreams, and probably will continue to do so well into the evening. On the far right another occupant of the house comes running out to greet the visitors. Who is she? A younger sister of the two women in the center perhaps, or a neighbor who has stopped by for a cup of coffee?

Note, too, the setting of the painting is high above the town below, giving it a safely removed perspective even though the town seems clean and well-kept and at least modestly prosperous and not a threat to the idyllic panorama. In addition, the full-figured persons Mattison presents for our viewing, ranging from the chubby baby to the busty young woman on the right, indicate a comfortable existence, if not an affluent one.

The Section officials, although they had a few minor suggestions—omit a rose arbor, check the relationship of one figure to another—had admiration and praise for the artist's efforts from the very beginning. Mattison's first pencil drawing was called "particularly interesting," and the color sketch was "quite handsome." Perhaps both the Section administrators and the artist were acting cautiously in making critical comments and in the responses to suggestions, after Mattison's Tipton undertaking the year before, when he prepared three designs because he thought the comments from the Washington office meant the preceding ones were not acceptable.

When he sent the photograph of the full-size cartoon to Washington, Mattison noted that it was "still in a workable condition in the event of your making further suggestions." Rowan's reply a few days later is one of the most glowing of any in the files of the Section:

> I wish I could let you know of the complete enthusiasm in this office for the fine way in which you have developed this work. The cartoon is beautiful in drawing and the figures possess extremely handsome characterization which I trust you will be able to retain in the finished work. The central group of figures is in my opinion a distinguished achievement in drawing and arrangement.

Perhaps the highest compliment for Mattison's work came from the most important segment of all, the viewing public. When the postmaster wrote to confirm the satisfactory installation of the mural, he commented that "this painting is a real work of art which adds much to the decoration of the building and has aroused much favorable comment from patrons of this office."

Donald M. Mattison also painted *Indiana Farming* for Tipton in 1937.

FROM THE PHOTOGRAPHER'S PERSPECTIVE

In the spring of 1992 Kent Calder, managing editor of *Traces of Indiana and Midwestern History,* called me about an article in progress on Indiana's post office murals. John C. Carlisle had researched the murals extensively, producing an article, a video, and a slide presentation. Kent asked if I would be interested in photographing certain murals with my large format cameras, which yield results suitable for full- and double-page reproductions in magazines.

Kent and I met and watched John's slide program, studying the imagery in the murals. We selected eight murals to represent the variety of imagery: Garrett, Nappanee, Spencer, Lafayette, Crawfordsville, Aurora, Cambridge City, and Broad Ripple. Kent needed the transparencies within four weeks, so I began to plan my route.

I had often photographed paintings, T. C. Steele's for example, and I always used a 1945 Deardorf camera that had a 4 x 5-inch format. This particular camera is made of wood and has an 18-inch bellows. A variety of lenses can be used, each lens having the ability to be moved up or down or tilted or turned, in order to produce a distortion-free image. Since I had photographed smaller paintings I had the necessary experience to work with flat-field, two dimensional objects. Now I had to utilize that experience and apply it to the large-scale murals.

Since I was an Owen County resident, I decided to "practice" with the mural in Spencer and learn what types of difficulties I might expect to encounter. If the first photographs did not work, I could always repeat the process until I had it right. Fortunately, or unfortunately, everything went too smoothly, and I thought that I could complete the project on time and without any difficulties.

I explained the project to the Spencer postmaster, who immediately gave me permission and asked if I needed any help. All that I needed was a ladder. I decided to use only the natural light that came in through the windows, feeling that this would best convey what people would see when they went to the post office. The Spencer mural is fourteen feet long and five feet high and is above the doorway to the postmaster's office. This puts the middle of the mural at a height of approximately ten feet, so I placed the camera at the same height and in the middle of the room since the mural covered the entire length of the wall.

The Spencer post office has a wooden vestibule inside the entrance, as do most of the other post offices. I placed the tripod in front of it and used a lens suitable for the distance. This type of vestibule pre-

sented a problem at subsequent post offices since it often extended into the middle of the room, which is exactly where I wanted to place the tripod. Also, the height of most of the vestibules is about eight feet, so I needed a ladder that would place the camera at a height above its ceiling. Most of the post offices have government-issued ladders with small platforms. I placed a Gitzo tripod with the 4 x 5 Deardorf onto the platform while standing on the steps and viewed the image on the ground glass at the back of the camera.

This type of camera is called a "view camera" because one can view the image directly as it passes through the lens and falls upon the ground glass of the camera. The only problem is that the image is upside down and reversed left to right. In order to see the mural and to focus the lens, I drape a large black cloth over my head. This prevents any extraneous light from coming in, but it also raises questions in the mind of anyone present: "What are you doing under there? What are you looking at?"

My chief goal was to portray the murals accurately and without distortion, and I used the view camera to its fullest extent, moving the lens or the camera back in order to place the mural's image correctly on the ground glass. Sometimes a lens was raised two inches above the normal position; at other times the lens or the back was moved laterally left or right. Because my eyes can no longer focus at close range, I used a magnifier to see the image clearly on the ground glass. This process is also invaluable since the light reaching the corners is often insufficient, and it is important that the corners of the image are sharply focused.

After the focusing stage is completed, the next step is to close the shutter and place the film holder in the camera. But before I can trip the shutter I have to measure the light. The camera lens has both a shutter speed and an opening that allow different quantities of light onto the film, and each needs to be set in combination relative to the available light. I tried to use either f/16 or f/22 as the opening and would vary the shutter speed according to the light conditions. To determine the proper light setting I used two different types of meters: an incident meter that measures the amount of light that falls on the subject (the mural and the meter); and a one degree spot meter that reads the amount of light reflected off the mural. These two meters gave widely divergent readings, so it took an interpretation of each of their characteristics to determine the correct combination of the shutter speed and aperture. Once this was determined and the lens was set, the final step was to remove the dark slide, which covers the film, and to trip the shutter. While it seems a simple task I learned that it sometimes would be the longest.

If the day was clear and bright, the light level remained constant, resulting in a simple last step. However, most sunny days can have white cumulus clouds that block the sun with varying degrees of density. Sometimes I had the shutter cocked, the dark slide out of the film holder, and my hands on the cable release ready to push the plunger— then a discernible drop in the light would occur. The bright light would change from abundance to insufficiency. Not only would there be a difference in how the mural appeared, but less light would also

mean a longer exposure—and a longer exposure leads to reciprocity failure in the film. At longer than normal times (20–30 seconds) film is not sensitively proportional, and so an exposure meter time of 20 seconds would require an actual time of 30–45 seconds. A 30-second meter time requires a 60-second actual time, and a 60-second meter reading requires a 150-second actual exposure. Of course, all of this varies according to the type of film used because there is no standard law of reciprocity failure for all films. Only testing can tell you what is the correct exposure.

This means that the light coming in the window is critical, making a sunny day preferable to a cloudy day. Trying to determine how many absolutely clear, sunny days there are and predicting them as I traveled across the state became a real challenge. For example, if I leave Spencer at sunrise, it will take me five hours to reach Nappanee, and a clear, sunny day can change into a cloudy day the farther north I travel. I am always conscious of the weather as a determining factor in taking photographs and try to work with its variables.

Although I started with the 1945 4 x 5 Deardorf, I subsequently changed to a 1928 Deardorf 4 x 5 Special because it is a larger view camera that can accommodate a 5 x 7-inch format. I had worked with a 1950s Burke and James 6 x 17 cm film back and had Benjamin Queary adapt it to the Deardorf. This film back produces four exposures on a roll of 120 film; each frame is 6 x 17 cm in size (2¼ x 7 inches), giving an image ratio of approximately 3 to 1. This proved to be the perfect format for the long post office murals as the murals would fill the entire frame, thereby giving a much larger transparency from which to print.

The initial photographs at the Spencer post office were successful, and I embarked on the mural journey with confidence. It took only one other mural to prove that I had not encountered any real difficulties at Spencer, and that I would meet new and unusual problems and frustrations at almost every post office. There was no assurance that this would be an easy undertaking, but I could be assured of a unique challenge awaiting me at every post office. My confidence could rest only on my ability to solve the technical problems.

The next mural I attempted was at the Broad Ripple post office. I entered the lobby thinking that I could just set up the ladder and tripod as I had at Spencer. However, I found a light suspended from the ceiling in such a way that it appeared directly in front of the mural. If I took the photograph from the middle of the lobby by the vestibule the lamp would block much of the mural. I needed to be in front of the lamp, but that would put me too close to the mural. I returned home

to Owen County and came back, when the weather permitted, with a wide-angle lens, a 65 mm Super Angulon. With that lens I hoped to photograph the entire mural while being between the mural and the ceiling lamp. It eventually worked, but I had to have the camera body touching the lamp, and I kept bumping the lamp with my head.

The photography at Crawfordsville and Lafayette was relatively straightforward, but photographing the mural at Nappanee proved to be a bigger challenge. The post office at Nappanee did not have a sufficient size ladder to place the camera above the vestibule. To solve this dilemma I used the Deardorf camera and the 6 x 17 panoramic back to their fullest capabilities. I set the lens and back swing to its most angular setting and placed the camera near the wall. The lens was off-axis and the camera bellows twisted in such a way that I could keep both the lens and the film back parallel to, yet not lined up directly in front of, the mural. The image on the ground glass showed the mural in its entirety, but a viewer on observing the camera angle would conclude that it was not aiming at the mural. This is the beauty of the view camera—the bellows allows both the lens and the back to be moved to great extremes in order to produce a desired result.

I concluded from these first murals that I should use the 1928 Deardorf with the panoramic back because its 6 x 17 cm (3 to 1 ratio) image coincided with the dimensions of most of the murals. Also, I knew that I would have to purchase the largest tripod available in order to place the camera above the height of most of the vestibules (eight feet), and I was able to buy a tripod that would extend to nine feet. Not all of the post offices had the same type of ladder, so I needed a ladder to accompany the tripod. Randy Tomasino kindly loaned me an eight-foot ladder. I packed all of this equipment into a small Honda Civic!

When Kent Calder called me two years later about photographing all of the post office murals throughout the state I knew that I was ready for such a task. While I thought I knew what to expect in the way of difficulties, I was unprepared and unequipped to photograph many of the murals on the first visit. For example, when I arrived at the post office in Angola I discovered that the original post office was closed. When I reached the new location I learned that the mural was not there but was on a wall at the old high school, which had been converted into a community center. The mural was covered with glass and placed in a dimly lit hallway, too dark to take the photograph with available light. Six months later I returned to Angola with portable lights, extension cords, and film balanced for tungsten lighting.

Twice I arrived at a post office and found ceiling lamps suspended in such a way that I could not use the bellows movement on the camera and avoid the lamp. I photographed the murals from a low elevation and angled the camera in such a way that the murals would appear distorted in the transparency. This distortion was corrected by a computer graphics program that straightens angled lines. The postmaster of the Lagrange post office personally removed the offending ceiling light.

It must have been a strange sight for customers coming into the post office to see a camera perched on a nine-foot tripod and a person standing on a ladder with his head hidden by a large black cloth. Oftentimes someone would ask me what I was photographing, and I would say something about the historical importance of the large mural. To my surprise many people would ask me when the mural was placed there, remarking that they had never seen it. When I answered that the mural had been there for over fifty years, they could not believe that they had never noticed it before. Others, however, mentioned that they remembered seeing the mural as children when they would go to the post office with their parents.

Some of the murals have a dull, dark look to them from fifty years of accumulated dust and smoke. Some murals have been restored, and they look brighter and more colorful. I hoped to convey exactly what the murals look like now, so I had to accept their present condition, whatever it was. My challenge was to photograph the murals in an undistorted, clear manner so that the reader of this book could appreciate their beauty. I hope that many people will want to travel and see the murals with their own eyes.

Darryl Jones

Allen, Frederick Lewis. *Since Yesterday*. New York: Bantam, 1961.

"America Sees Itself in New Government Murals," *Life,* 27 January 1941, 42–44.

Baigell, Matthew. *The American Scene*. New York: Praeger, 1974.

Bulletin, Number 1. Washington, D.C.: Section of Painting and Sculpture, Public Works Branch, Procurement Division, Treasury Department, 1 March 1935.

————, Number 3. Washington, D.C.: Section of Painting and Sculpture, Public Works Branch, Procurement Division, Treasury Department, 1 May 1935.

————, Number 4. Washington, D.C.: Section of Painting and Sculpture, Public Works Branch, Procurement Division, Treasury Department, 1 June 1935.

————, Number 20. Washington, D.C.: Section of Fine Arts, Public Buildings Administration, Federal Works Agency, November 1939.

Kaeser, William. Interview with the author, 26 May 1978.

McKinzie, Richard D. *The New Deal for Artists*. Princeton: Princeton University Press, 1973.

Marling, Karal Ann. *Wall-to-Wall America: A Cultural History of Post-Office Murals in the Great Depression*. Minneapolis: University of Minnesota Press, 1982.

Meltzer, Milton. *Violins and Shovels: The WPA Art Projects*. New York: Delacorte, 1976.

Morse, John D. "Ben Shahn: An Interview," *Magazine of Art* (April 1944): 136–41.

O'Connor, Francis V. *Federal Support for the Visual Arts: The New Deal and Now*. New York: New York Graphic Society, 1969.

Park, Marlene, and Gerald Markowitz. *Democratic Vistas: Post Offices and Public Art in the New Deal*. Philadelphia: Temple University Press, 1984.

"Records of the Public Building Service." RG 121, National Archives and Records Service, Washington, D.C.

Rose, Barbara. *American Art since 1900: A Critical History*. New York: Praeger, 1967.

Shahn, Ben. Letter to the author, 14 February 1969.

"Speaking of Pictures . . . This Is Mural America for Rural Americans," *Life,* 4 December 1939, 12–13, 16.

Stewart, Rick. *Lone Star Regionalism: The Dallas Nine and Their Circle*. Austin: Texas Monthly Press, 1985.

Tompkins, Alan. Interview with the author, 15 July 1978.

"Winners in Government's '48-States Competition' Shown at Corcoran," *The Art Digest* (15 November 1939): 12.

DESIGNER:
Dean Johnson Design, Inc.,
Indianapolis, Indiana

TYPEFACE:
Berkeley

TYPOGRAPHER:
Weimer Graphics,
Indianapolis, Indiana

PAPER:
70-pound Cougar Opaque
Smooth, Book Weight

PRINTER:
Shepard Poorman
Communications Corporation,
Indianapolis, Indiana